COGNITION, COMPUTERS AND CREATIVE WRITING

ELLIS HORWOOD SERIES IN COGNITIVE SCIENCE
Series Editor: Masoud Yazdani, University of Exeter

COMPUTER EXPERIENCE AND COGNITIVE DEVELOPMENT: A Child's Learning in a Computer Culture
R. LAWLER, G.T.E. Laboratories Inc., USA
COGNITION, COMPUTERS AND CREATIVE WRITING
M. SHARPLES, University of Sussex

COGNITION, COMPUTERS AND CREATIVE WRITING

MIKE SHARPLES, B.Sc., Ph.D.
Lecturer in Artificial Intelligence
University of Sussex

ELLIS HORWOOD LIMITED
Publishers · Chichester

Halsted Press: a division of
JOHN WILEY & SONS
New York · Chichester · Brisbane · Toronto

First published in 1985 by

ELLIS HORWOOD LIMITED

Market Cross House, Cooper Street, Chichester, West Sussex, PO19 1EB, England

The publisher's colophon is reproduced from James Gillison's drawing of the ancient Market Cross, Chichester.

Distributors:

Australia, New Zealand, South-east Asia:
Jacaranda-Wiley Ltd., Jacaranda Press,
JOHN WILEY & SONS INC.,
G.P.O. Box 859, Brisbane, Queensland 4001, Australia

Canada:
JOHN WILEY & SONS CANADA LIMITED
22 Worcester Road, Rexdale, Ontario, Canada.

Europe, Africa:
JOHN WILEY & SONS LIMITED
Baffins Lane, Chichester, West Sussex, England.

North and South America and the rest of the world:
Halsted Press: a division of
JOHN WILEY & SONS
605 Third Avenue, New York, N.Y. 10158 U.S.A.

© **1985 M. Sharples/Ellis Horwood Limited**

British Library Cataloguing in Publication Data
Sharples, M.
Cognition, computers and creative writing. —
(Ellis Horwood series in cognitive science)
1. Creative writing (Elementary education) — Computer assisted instruction
2. Creative writing (Secondary education) — Computer assisted instruction
I. Title
808'.042'078   LB1576

Library of Congress Card No. 85–21921

ISBN 0–85312–895–2 (Ellis Horwood Limited)
ISBN 0–470–20261–0 (Halsted Press)

Typeset by Ellis Horwood Limited
Printed in Great Britain by Unwin Brothers of Woking

Table of Contents

Foreword

Mike Sharples describes an exploration by schoolchildren of territory which is not only unfamiliar but, for many, forbidding also. This territory is the child's own language, in its written form.

Writing is difficult. Even when a child can effortlessly produce legible handwriting, she still has to decide which ideas are relevant. She has to decide also how those ideas should be expressed: but how can she choose sensibly between different ways of saying the same thing, unless she knows the range of possible alternatives?

The teaching of writing-skills is difficult too. It risks being either too abstract or too unstructured. One can try to teach grammar, and lose sight of content and style, or one can encourage the child to 'do her own thing' while offering little guidance on what sorts of 'things' might possibly be done, and how.

This book describes a way of teaching children to write that leads them to enjoy exploring the possibilities provided by their language, and which provides inbuilt maps, guides, and compasses to help them do so fruitfully. The computer-environment by Sharples is a tool for play, for learning, and for creativity. His pupils — by no means 'bookish' types — came to delight in producing their own newspaper, or in writing poems good enough to be included in their school magazine.

It's not Proust — but it is a first step, in an area where too many children in our schools today fail even to reach the starting-line.

Margaret A. Boden

Preface

In 1977, when I joined the Department of Artificial Intelligence at Edinburgh University as a research student, there was a project in progress to investigate children learning mathematics through the Logo programming language. Two of the children on the project, both 15-year-old boys, had been working with Logo for over a year and had become bored with writing programs to draw patterns on the screen, so I suggested some projects that might engage their imagination. These included linking Logo to motors to control machinery, writing programs to generate music, exploring the paths of simulated moving objects such as bouncing balls, and writing programs to produce poems. To my surprise both boys chose the poem project.

We worked as a team, with the boys specifying the programs which I then coded in Logo. They began by generating words at random and then added constraints of grammar and meaning, looking through books of poetry to discover the patterns, rhythms and vocabulary of poems, and attempting to distil these into Logo. After some ten hourly sessions over two school terms, the boys reached the goal they had set at the start: three of their Logo poems were published in the school magazine. Their enthusiasm for the project, their use of the computer as an exploratory tool, and the skills they gained in controlling language all warranted further investigation. This book is a record of that investigation, which resulted in a computer-based teaching scheme for language exploration and creative writing that was tested with a small group of 11-year-old children.

Eight years ago, the computer in secondary education was the preserve of mathematics and science teachers; the few available computer programs for language arts were almost entirely tedious drill and practise exercises. We are now in an interesting transition period, with software magazines still advertising drill programs with lurid titles like 'Spell Invader' and 'Verb Viper', but also a growing awareness that children can benefit from powerful tools such as word processors, reference aids, story planners and ideas organisers. In order to design, explain and assess such tools we need to know how people learn: their cognitive development, acquisition of new skills and processes of problem solving and creativity. The book is more about children's minds and writing than it is about computers, and that reflects my own preoccupation of the past eight years.

I should like to thank all those who helped me sort out ideas and transform them into words. Jim Howe and Ben du Boulay supervised the research. They, along with Geoff Cumming and Helen Pain commented on earlier drafts and provided valuable advice. I am indebted to Tim O'Shea, for helping me through the early stages of the research, to Bill Clocksin, for advice on programming, to the two teachers who marked the children's essays, to Chris Miller, for adapting the FANTASY program to my specification, to Helen Finlayson and Andre Wagstaff for the Logo documentation and to the Economic and Social Research Council for financial support. My thanks also to Masoud Yazdani and Michael Horwood for guiding me through the final stages.

I owe particular thanks to the children of Primay 7, South Bridge School, and to their teacher Mrs. Findlayson. Their enthusiasm carried me over the long period between project and book.

1

Introduction

Speech belongs to everyone. It is through verbal language that we exchange experience, organise ideas and win friends. Not so writing. Writing is the medium through which society's values are expressed, its literary culture recorded, its shared knowledge stored. To contribute to this storehouse requires access to technology – pen, typewriter, printing press – and the greater and more lasting the contribution, the more expensive and exclusive the machinery. Children have little hold on these resources and consequently their view of the world is largely missing from recorded history, or at best has been collated and reworked by adults. Children do realise the power of written language and they attempt to lay claim to it, through graffiti, poems, diaries and stories.

> Learning to write is one of the few school activities which students rate
> as highly in importance as their teachers do. In a recent Hull enquiry,
> virtually all second and third year pupils across the ability range said
> that they thought it was 'very important'. (Protherough, 1983).

To be a writer is empowering, yet every word that a child forms on paper is a confirmation of inferiority. However carefully and neatly a child may write, the result is a poor substitute for adult typeface. If we want children to become adult writers, we should equip them with adult writing tools.

Machinery to create presentable text is one kind of tool, but if a child is to command the full range and power of the written word then she also needs tools for reasoning: a simple meta-language with which to talk about thought and language, an appreciation of the patterns in text, and an understanding of the process of writing. Piaget and other developmental psychologists have shown that by the age of eleven or twelve children are able to think abstractly and can divorce language from its immediate context, so that it becomes an object to be mentally shaped and revised. They acquire this awareness as part of normal cognitive development:

> The adolescent (eleven to fifteen) can reason abstractly, since she can formally conceptualize possible transformations and their results (instead of having to imagine them figuratively or carry them out physically). That is, she can apply operations to operations, so that she can reason about her own reasoning independently of figurative (e.g. perceptual or semantic) content. (Boden, 1979, p. 74).

Furthermore, children are not passive recipients of knowledge, but are actively engaged in interpreting their surroundings, searching for the rules underlying both natural phenomena and human constructs and integrating these with existing cognitive structures. They enjoy playing games with language so as to discover its form. The notion that writing is a cognitive process, open to conscious inspection, manipulation and control, is relatively recent. Even *Elements of Style* (Strunk and White, 1979), that assured guide to good writing, asks:

> Who can confidently say what ignites a certain combination of words, causing them to explode in the mind? . . . These are high mysteries . . .
> There is no satisfactory explanation of style, no infallible guide to good writing, no assurance that a person who thinks clearly will be able to write clearly, no key that will unlock the door.

Writing no longer remains a 'high mystery'. Research in cognition and linguistics promises to provide a comprehensive and applicable theory of text creation, one that can help a child to develop the skills of creative writing in a conscious and systematic manner.

Conscious attention is a slow, limited, single-channel process and we would not be able to walk and talk, sing and dance, if we were constantly debating the choice of a word while planning where to place a foot. Some mental activities, like interpreting visual images, are permanently hidden from self-inspection; others, like language production, lie in the boundaries of awareness. For these *boundary skills,* the human mind has an astonishing ability to switch between intuitive processing and conscious deliberation. Furthermore having both a conscious (or *declarative*) and intuitive (*compiled*) understanding of a complex skill can be a help in acquiring, evaluating and integrating new techniques. This has important implications for teaching and one boundary skill where it has been successfully applied is sports training. Much of the modern training method of an athlete, ice skater or gymnast is concerned with describing and analysing a routine, breaking it down into individual movements, rehearsing the difficult ones, adding new actions and then rebuilding a polished performance. The method includes:

Meta-language
Terms must be adopted or invented to describe the relevant movements and styles and every sport has a complex language with esoteric terms like 'barani' or 'double toe loop' to permit discussion between performer and coach.

Plateaus

Progress is not smooth and gradual. Austin (1974), in describing a project to train novices to juggle, comments:

> The single most surprising discovery made during the experiment was that for most individuals progress . . . was not at all continuous but, rather, appeared to consist of a series of breakthroughs or plateaus. These breakthroughs were not initially stable, frequently being attainable for only one or two trials, but became more frequent and stable over time.

The implication for teaching is that the coach should be more concerned with detecting and fostering 'breakthroughs' than pushing forward every aspect of performance.

Restructuring

This is an essential period of learning, when the emphasis is not on overall quality, but exploring ideas and achieving new styles and techniques.

Assistance

At times during the restructuring period a learner will need physical assistance, that allows her to concentrate on one specific movement while neglecting others. A tennis coach, for instance, may toss up the ball for a learner to practice service strokes.

Encouragement

A coach who concentrates on errors and problems can cause a learner to practise only those skills she performs badly, with consequent loss of confidence. Modern sports coaching builds on success by encouragement.

Diagnostic Assessment

The learner and coach need to agree on clear criteria by which to judge both the overall performance and its important features.

Practice

A learner needs ample opportunity to try out and compile new routines in a realistic context for a variety of audiences.

The cognitive processes involved in creative writing and in physical performance are sufficiently similar that, for example, the 'plateaus' of progress described by Austin have been discovered (with equal surprise) by observers of children's writing development. The major British Government report on the teaching of English in Schools, the Bullock Report (Department of Education and Science, 1975), contains the following recommendation:

> Pupils should be given the opportunity to write for a variety of readers and audiences. They should be faced with the need to analyse the

specific task, to choose the language appropriate to it and to establish the criteria by which to judge what they have achieved. (p. 527).

The statement, and others in the concluding section of the Report, gave authority to a new approach to the teaching of English, combining descriptive linguistics with a cognitive theory of writing, that resembles the sports coaching method described above. This book takes up the Bullock recommendation by describing a teaching scheme for creative writing that takes account of a child's developing cognitive abilities. The scheme is in two parts. The first develops the child's explicit knowledge of language and equips her with a small active vocabulary of linguistic terms. The child explores structure and constraint in language, is introduced to grammar as a productive system, and expands her active vocabulary of linguistic terms. This lays a foundation for the second part of the scheme, in which the child experiments with new styles and techniques for creative writing.

The links between cognition and creative writing are clear, but the inclusion of 'computers' in the book's title is less obvious. The computer is the equivalent of 'physical assistance' in sports coaching. A child with a word processor can concentrate on planning a story and turning ideas into text, while leaving consideration of spelling, punctuation and sentence layout to a second pass. The result will always be presentable and worthy of comparison with printed text. The computer can also model the rules and processes of language and offer these models to children in the form of powerful and general learning aids: a sentence generator; a story planner and 'Adventure Game' creator; a text editor and transformer; an automated thesaurus. Computers form an integral part of the pilot teaching scheme which was tested with eleven-year-old children over 29 sessions of 60–70 minutes' duration.

Chapters 2 and 3 investigate a child's development of writing abilities and the writing process of both adults and children, proposing 'feature analysis' as a method of detecting short-term developments in a child's written product. Chapter 4 is a critical survey of the teaching of writing in schools and a review of computer software relevant to English teaching. Chapter 5 describes the design and operation of the computer programs used in the teaching scheme. All detail of the programs has been left to this chapter and, although computer jargon is avoided wherever possible, some knowledge of a computer language, such as Basic or preferably Logo, would be a useful prerequisite to reading it. Chapter 7 recounts the progress of the six children who took part in the project, describing the teaching sessions, their use of the computers and the changes in their writing process. It also contains an assessment of the essays, produced as pre and post tests by the experimental group and an equivalent control group of children. The last chapter is devoted to suggestions for future research and possible applications of the teaching scheme and methods of assessment.

2

A Child's development of writing abilities

(1) I am standing near the Surfer, watching all of the people paying, then climbing into the empty cars, then it starting up and everybody screaming and the loud music, children eating toffee apples and Candy Floss holding flags and balloons. It is getting late the children leave and only adults are left to spend money.

The ghost train goes in and you hear screaming, then out comes frightened passengers. Only a few people remain now, the screams die down, the shows pack away, only a few people remain, walking, through the quiet empty shows that will be alive once more.

I remembered the penny arcade, the children shouting, winning money, losing money, I remembered how the people screamed on the big wheel which they would do again the next day.

(2) The long tunnel under the parade was the noisiest, lowest, cheapest section of Brighton's amusements. Children rushed past them in paper sailor-caps marked 'I'm no Angel'; a ghost train rattled by carrying courting couples into a squealing and shrieking darkness. All the way along the landward side of the tunnel were the amusements; on the other little shops: Magpie Ices, Photoweigh, Shellfish, Rocko. The shelves rose to the ceiling: little doors let you into the obscurity behind, and on the sea side were no doors at all, no windows, nothing but shelf after shelf from the pebbles to the roof: a breakwater of Brighton rock facing the sea. The lights were always on in the tunnel; the air was warm and thick and poisoned with human breath.

The two extracts given above are both on the same theme – a description of a fairground – and both are approximately the same length. Neither contains gross technical errors of syntax, punctuation, or spelling. Yet the first is clearly written by a child (Anne, aged 11) and the second by a skilled adult writer (the extract is from *Brighton Rock* by Graham Greene (Greene, 1970, pp. 177–178)). What does the first passage contain that identifies it as a piece of child's prose? How can a child develop her writing abilities to match those of an accomplished adult? And what of poor adult writers? Is their prose similar to that of an expert writer, perhaps lacking in polish and vocabulary, or are their language styles and structures more like those of a child?

2.1 WRITING DEVELOPMENT

By the age of 9 or 10, children 'possess the core of language resources' (Harpin, 1976, p. 53) and, in general, produce text that is well-formed and has all the essential grammatical structures (Hunt, 1965). Nevertheless, children's writing differs markedly in style and structure from mature adult prose. A simple explanation of writing development, one cherished by many school teachers, is that children gradually acquire more mature language through reading and practice in composition. If this were the only process then the writing of children taught together should develop at roughly the same rate. Harpin examined the writing of 290 children over six school terms and concluded:

> If age and practice were the only influences, the written language of any one 9-year-old would be much like that of any other. Children exposed to the same classroom environment would move forward more or less identically. Yet the reality is very different. Some children seem to advance very little over considerable periods of time . . . Others appear to mark time for months and then accelerate with startling rapidity to overhaul their peers. (Harpin, 1976, p. 74.)

Nor is there a steady age-related trend in writing taken from a group of children. Kidder studied the writing of children at six grade levels (ages 5.9–12.8), with approximately 20 children in each group. She found that:

> The pattern of [syntactic] development by age is generally one of increasing complexity in syntax, with one noted regression at the period 9.9–10.8 [years] . . . The analysis of vocabulary intensity of children's writing resulted in some curiosity-provoking patterns. There was evidence of increases in intensity in early years, plateaus or regressions in the middle years, and then an award curve again in upper elementary years. (Kidder, 1974, pp. 89–90).

Kidder suggests that:

> [The study] has raised some interesting questions about patterns of language development in children. Further investigation of these patterns in children's writing should be made. The observed plateaus need to be studied. An attempt to identify the correlation between the patterns

observed and stages described in learning theories such as Piaget's might be worthwhile. (Kidder, 1974, p. 93).

It appears that a child's process of writing is very different from that of an adult. As a child matures, she passes through stages of linguistic development related to the Piagetian stages of cognitive development and these changes affect the quality of a child's writing. Thus, to understand children's writing development we need to look closely at their development of language and thought.

2.1.1 Linguistic and meta-linguistic development

Gleitman and her colleagues (Gleitman, Gleitman and Shipley, 1972) have investigated the linguistic skills of young children. Their work, along with that of Bohannon (1976) and Slobin (1971), suggests several clear stages of linguistic and meta-linguistic development:

Stage 1:
The child utters sounds and single words, but produces no grammatical patterns.

Stage 2:
Speech conforms to the rules of a series of increasingly complex grammars.

Stage 3:
The child is able to recognise ambiguous and deviant sentences — the first signs of meta-linguistic abilities. Gleitman reports an experiment in which three subjects, all aged two-and-a-half, were asked to judge spoken sentences as 'good' or 'silly'. In some of the sentences the order of the noun and verb were reversed ('Ball me the bring'; 'Ball bring'). 'For all subjects, the reversed order sentences result in more judgements of silly.'

Stage 4:
Tacit rule knowledge: the child is able to discuss deviant examples of language in terms of particular linguistic rules, but is able to refer to the rules only by example. For example, a child, aged 8, is being asked to comment on the grammatical correctness of sentences (Gleitman, Gleitman and Shipley, 1972):

> Experimenter: How about this one: 'Boy is at the door'?
> Child: (That's OK) if his name is 'Boy'. The kid is named 'John', see?
> 'John is at the door' or 'A boy is at the door' or 'He's knocking at the door'.

Stage 5:
Explicit rule knowledge: the child is able to formulate and apply general rules. A 15-year-old boy (Sharples, 1978):

> 'You need a 'the' before an object'.

Gleitman's study indicates that by the age of 9–10[†], her subjects were aware of the rules governing language structure and this ability appears to be closely related to the Piagetian stage of *formal operations*:

[†]The report stresses that the subjects were particularly able children: 'we have taken some pains to interview children we suspected were highly articulate'.

The adolescent's theory construction shows both that he has become more capable of reflective thinking and that his thought makes it possible for him to escape the concrete present toward the abstract and the possible. (Inhelder and Piaget, 1958, p. 342).

The statement describes accurately the activity of Gleitman's eight-year-old subject. She is not concerned about the empirical truth of the statement ('Boy is at the door'), but about its conformity to grammatical rules. She has clearly been able to understand the concept represented by the deviant structure and has then generated three syntactically different sentences to express that concept.

An early study by Piaget, of children's behaviour while playing marbles, shows a clear similarity between meta-linguistic development and the acquisition of game rules:

As to the child's behavioural conformity to the rules, the stages appeared to be as follows. In Stage 1, the child uses marbles simply as free-play materials, without any attempt to adapt to social rules. At most, the child develops private rituals of play which might be called 'motor rules'. Stage 2 (about 3–5 years) begins when the child imitates aspects of rule-regulated play behaviour of his elders. However, it is clear that the child assimilates what he sees to private, egocentric schemas; confident that he is playing by older children's rules, he nonetheless plays in an idiosyncratic, socially isolated manner, unintentionally flouting the rules at every turn. From about 7–8 years on, the child begins to play the game in a genuinely social way, in accordance with a mutually agreed on set of rules. But until about age 11–12, this grasp and conformity to the rules is still vague and approximate (Stage 3). From 11–12 on, however, they are completely understood and obeyed to the letter by all (Stage 4); moreover the act of codifying rules now seems to have a positive fascination for the child, e.g. he is constantly engaged on revising the statutes to cover new and unforeseen contingencies. (Flavell, 1963, pp. 291–292).

These stages of rule-following behaviour appear to match the linguistic stages, with 'explicit rule knowledge' corresponding to the 'act of codifying rules'.

The nature of validity of Piagetian states is a matter for debate. Researchers have replicated some of Piaget's experiments, varying the subject matter and method of presentation, and have found no simple correspondence between a child and a stage. For example, a child's performance in a class inclusion task may be influenced by the presentation of the experimental material, or the wording of the instructions. The child may show operational thinking in one experiment but not in another isomorphic, but differently presented, experiment (Donaldson, 1978a, pp. 48–50).

We do not, however, suggest that there is an exact correspondence between the growth of meta-linguistic knowledge and Piagetian stages of cognitive development, nor that a child will show the same linguistic ability at all levels of text and for all writing topics, merely that Piaget's developmental theory helps us to explain both the linguistic structure of child and adult writing and children's written language development.

From the age of about four onwards, a child is able to write text that con-forms to the rules of grammar, but she borrows production techniques and linguistic structures from conversation. Although she learns some conventions appropriate to writing, such as spelling, punctuation, and simple rules of style, her 'grasp and conformity to the rules is still vague and approximate'. Then as part of her natural cognitive development around the age of 9—11, the child becomes aware of her own thought and language and begins to take command of her writing.

Bereiter and Scardamalia (1982) have investigated children's writing develop-ment and suggest that there is no easy progression from a writing process based on conversation to mature reflective writing, but rather a major reconstruction of thought and language. The development of mature writing abilities requires several important transitions:

(1) from self-directed expression to communication with a remote audience. The writer must create and sustain a model of the intended reader and be aware that the reader may not share the non-linguistic context of the writing. A child who writes about 'my family' for a school magazine should be aware that few readers will have her knowledge of the essay subject and that she may need to supply background information, such as character description or family history.

(2) from language production which is dependent on conversational feedback to autonomous production. The structure of a spoken conversation is guided by the conversational partners, but:

> in written composition all the supports are removed. This makes written compostion not only a harder task than conversation, it makes it a radically different kind of task. (Bereiter and Scarda-malia, 1982, p.2).

The writer must learn to generate language without the aid of encourage-ment, memory aids and grammatical support from a conversational partner.

(3) from open to closed discourse — speech is structured as it progresses, by the interplay of dialogue between the speakers and generally has no prearranged form or finishing point. Written composition is much more the result of of premeditation, with a structure and conclusion that may be planned in advance by the author.

(4) from implicit to explicit manipulation of language — once the creation of language is taken outside the bounds of time then a writer can deliberately explore new writing techniques:

> The lasting character of print means that there is time to stop and think, so that the child has a chance to consider possibilities — a chance that he may never have had before. (Donaldson, 1978a, p. 95).

Around the age of 9 to 11, the child is in the throes of a cognitive upheaval. She is reading and writing with new insight, but with the burden of making sense of the patterns in prose. She is discovering that language has rules, styles and conventions, that it is both orderly and riddled with exceptions. In short, she is thinking too hard about her writing. However painful, the transition to rule knowledge of language is important. The child gains conscious control of language and, with it, the ability to alter her process of writing towards that of an accomplished writer. As Donaldson (1978b) points out:

> [a young child] is not much given to thinking about his thinking or his language, yet if he is to bring language under deliberate control he has to become more aware of them.

A number of researchers have investigated the writing process of children (Emig, 1971), (Bereiter and Scardamalia, 1982), (Graves, 1975) and adults (Flower and Hayes, 1979), (Somers, 1980), (Cooper and Matsuhasi, 1983) using the techniques of protocol analysis and continuous observation, for tasks ranging from structured expository writing to creative fiction. Their aim has been to move from an understanding of writing based solely on final product towards a theory of the process by which experienced and inexperienced writers produce text. Humes (1981) provides a good summary of recent research.

2.2 THE PROCESS OF WRITING

Studying the cognitive processes of people engaged in problem-solving tasks is a common preoccupation of cognitive psychologists. Newell and Simon (1972) proposed the technique of *protocol analysis* as a means of identifying the activities, ordered in time, which a subject engages in while performing a task. Flower and Hayes (1979) have used protocol analysis to study the writing process. They gave adult writers specific tasks and asked them to talk about their thoughts and actions while writing. Then, from transcripts of the writers' protocols, they attempted to classify the comments according to the type of writing activity, such as planning — 'I'll just make a list of topics now' — or editing — 'That's not the right word' — that each one described.

Other researchers have employed more informal methods, such as collecting anecdotal information from writers at work, and combined them with the findings of psycholinguists, discourse theorists and cognitive psychologists to build up a composite picture of the writing process. What follows is an attempt to derive a model of the writing process from these studies, plus my own observations of children and adults as writers. The model encompasses levels of proficiency from older child to accomplish adult and differences in ability are described in terms of constraints, levels of focus and the relative contributions of three writing procedures. It accounts only for narrative and descriptive writing, where a writer is asked to write a story on a set theme in a limited time, but could be extended to cover other modes of writing.

2.2.1 Text structure

A piece of text has embedded layers of structure, from the order of events in a story to the arrangement of letters in a word. It is important to note that the lower the level of structure, the easier it is to instantiate, or fill in, the entities.

A writer can choose between possible sentence constructions, say between an active or a passive sentence, by mentally generating and comparing examples: 'Which fits in better here, "The brick hit him on the head" or " He was hit on the head by a brick"?'. The writer does not need to know the terms 'active' and 'passive', nor the syntactic structures they represent; he merely needs to generate and compare instances of the structures. Given the limitations of human working memory, a writer cannot mentally hold instances of higher-level structures than a sentence, and so must either write out alternative versions, or compare uninstantiated structures in the form of named conceptual entities ('the introduction'; 'the paragraph describing the restaurant'). These impose restrictions on the text to be generated but do not necessarily specify a form of words.

We shall call an uninstantiated text structure, at any level, a *plan*, and any instantiation of a plan, a *draft*. Thus, the table of contents for this book constitutes a plan and versions of the text, including the final one which appears in print, are drafts.

2.2.2 Constraints

The act of writing is best described as the act of juggling a number of simultaneous constraints. This is in contrast to seeing it as a series of steps that add up to a finished product. (Flower and Hayes, 1979).

Constraints perform a number of functions: they ensure consistency of style and content, they restrict the search of memory involved in generating text, and they give a focus to the writing. A writer may set different types of constraint, either consciously, or implicitly by choosing a particular theme. By deciding on, say, a seafaring story the writer invokes, by default, a bundle of conventions about vocabulary, setting, character and plot that act to constrain the text.

Constraints fall into general categories, the most clearly identifiable being global attributes, structural plans, rules and landmarks. Global properties set the bounds of the writing, both of content (e.g. setting, characterisation, vocabulary) and form (e.g. layout, length). They remain in force throughout a section of text and direct the focus of writing. Structural plans specify an ordering of text elements, from the simple 'introduction; scene-setting; character description; action; conclusion' to a complex web of plots, counter-plots, and sub-plots. They may operate at any text level and they provide a framework on which to hang the text. Rules are extensions of the adages of style and grammar set down in textbooks on writing — 'start a paragraph with a reference to the preceding paragraph'; 'don't repeat words in close proximity' — and lie dormant until activated by a particular combination of words. The computing term for such lurking regulators is *demons*. Landmarks are unordered collections of items — events, references, quotations — that should appear at some point in the text.

Constraints are not all set at the start of writing. As the text builds up it will itself impose further restrictions of consistency. They are essential for coordinating the text and directing the writing, but they impose cognitive demands on the writer:

It is no wonder many people find writing difficult. It is the very nature of the beast to impose a large set of converging but potentially contra-dictory constraints on the writer. Furthermore, to be efficient the writer should attend to all of these constraints at once ... Unfortuna-tely, this ideal rarely occurs because of the limited number of items that short term memory or conscious attention can handle. (Flower and Hayes, 1979).

Flower and Hayes suggest a number of strategies for reducing cognitive strain such as throwing away constraints, combining constraints into groups, setting priorities and drawing on well learned techniques or plans. Two other methods are a) to use an external memory such as a written plan or list of topics and b) to pass over responsibility for some constraint satisfaction like spelling or layout to an automated system. Both of these are important to the design of computer-based aids for writers.

2.2.3 Production

We suggest that there are three fundamental procedures of writing — 'generate and select', 'verify' and 'transform and select' — which may be called upon to create and modify plans or drafts at any structural level. For Generate and Select the writer (a) produces one or more alternative text forms to express a common concept, (b) compares the text forms by their ability to satisfy the current constraints and (c) selects one or more suitable forms. It may be more or less deliberate depending on the skill of the writer, the level and complexity of the text and the number of alternatives. The procedure is made explicit in 'brain-storming' where the writer uses free association to generate a list of alternative ideas and then selects those ideas most suited to the topic.

To say that a writer 'generates one or more text forms to express a common concept' begs the question of how the writer manages to extract the appropriate pieces of text from memory. Cooper and Matsuhashi (1983) describe in some detail the process involved in generating sentence-level text. They present their description as a series of discrete actions, but stress that these are idealisations of the complex, pressured business of decision-making during composing.

The first step in producing a sentence is to formulate a proposition: to plan the message by searching memory and identifying one or more chunks of meaning appropriate to the current constraints. Retrieval of information from semantic memory is still an ill-understood cognitive process, partly because it takes place below the level of conscious awareness. The next stage involves choosing the people, objects and incidents to be included in the expression of the proposition: 'choosing a frame on which the sentence can be hung' (Chafe, 1977). The writer then generates a speech act for the proposition, determining the theme and emphasis of the sentence and connecting it to the previous text by pronoun referents or lexical cohesives such as ellipsis. Finally, the writer selects a particular form of words to express the complete proposition, choosing amongst synonyms, constructing grammatical form, with appropriate tense and word agreement, and stores it in working memory before transcribing it onto the page. Generating and selecting uninstantiated forms will require a similar process, without the final stages of speech act production but with looser constraints and thus more possible forms to be retrieved and compared. This may seem an over elaborate account of the generation of a single sentence but it does indicate the mental demands of creating text under constraint.

Verification involves matching text already created against the current constraints, to detect mismatches and incongruities that would be candidate for transformation. In Transform and Select the writer employs an *operator* to change one already-created text form to another. An example of a high-level operator is reordering a list of topic headings and of a low-level operator is changing a sentence from passive to active voice. The most important operator, one that can be applied at any stage of the writing, at any text level, is deletion. Deletion not only removes irrelevant or less important material, it may also set off another cycle of text generation and transformation as the writer replaces the deleted text. Transform and Select is a more deliberate procedure than Generate and Select; a writer must become a critical reader, identifying mismatches between constraints and text, before applying the transformations and judging the result.

Analysing writing in terms of these procedures breaks down the conventional demarcation of plan, draft and revise. To plan a story, then write a draft and then revise the text is certainly one logical way to proceed, but it is not the only way of good writing. The process can be iterative (an author may plan, draft and revise section by section) or recursive (revising the text may entail another pass through the process, involving further sessions of planning and drafting). To complicate matters further, a writer may revise plans before embarking on a first draft.

Given the description of writing as a constraint-influenced process of text generation, verification and transformation, we can now examine how this process is performed by expert and inexpert writers, using extracts from the protocols of four adult writers as illustration. In an investigation (conducted by Open University students), twenty adults were asked to write on the theme of 'Leaves Turning' for ten minutes. A panel of three people independently marked the pieces. The two writers with the lowest scores (A and B below) and the two with the highest scores (C and D) were selected as the non-experts and experts respectively. All four writers were mature students studying a third-level undergraduate course in cognitive psychology and so were well able to reason about their thought and language. All four were given thirty minutes to write a piece of fiction to the title 'A Night at Luigi's' and were asked to describe their thoughts and decisions during that period. The verbal protocols were transcribed and analysed to find common composing strategies. Eight categories of reported activity were identified:

Strategy

Discusses general composing strategies, e.g. 'So first of all you need to set the background'.

Plan

Sets the constraints and framework of the story, e.g. 'Luigi's will be an Italian restaurant'; 'He's going to spend the whole night at Luigi's without this person turning up'.

Text
Recites the text being written, e.g. 'I ate with great gusto, er great pleasure'.

Relate
Relates the text being written to the plan, e.g. 'I'm carrying on with the dialogue now because it's going to develop the plot'.

Recap
Describes already-written text, e.g. 'Now I've got so far. Gone in the restaurant. Done a bit of description'.

Revise
Describes a revision or intended revision to the text or plan, e.g. 'I'll change the restaurant, er, club to restaurant'.

Commentary
Comments on the text, e.g. 'This story's coming alive'.

Problem
Indicates a writing problem, e.g. 'I'm stuck . . . because I'm coming to a sequence that I don't know whether I should continue or not'.

The protocol of each writer was broken into segments corresponding to each of the above categories, plus any pause in speech longer than ten seconds. Comments on matters unrelated to the writing task were omitted. Segmenting the protocols was not a straightforward task, particularly in choosing amongst the 'Strategy', 'Plan' and 'Text' categories. That distinction, however, is not central to the discussion which follows. Table 2.1 shows the total number of mentions for each writer and category, followed by the percentage, for each pair of writers, of the total number of mentions.

Table 2.1 — Total reported activities for each writer.

	NON-EXPERTS			EXPERTS		
	A	B		C	D	
STRATEGY	2	7	14%	2	4	11%
PLAN	7	4	17%	2	4	11%
TEXT	12	11	32%	3	7	18%
RELATE	4	2	9%	4	9	23%
RECAP	0	2	3%	3	1	7%
REVISE	1	0	1%	2	3	10%
COMMENTARY	1	2	5%	1	1	4%
PROBLEM	2	8	15%	1	8	16%
TOTAL	29	36		18	37	

Three of the categories (Strategy, Plan and Text) can be considered as references to the process of Generate and Select. All these categories occurred on a higher percentage of occasions for the non-expert writers than the experts, the greatest difference being in references to the form of words in the text. The Revise category refers to Transform and Select and the protocols of the expert writers contained more instances from this category. Relate and Recap are descriptions of the Verify process and again the expert writers mention this more often. The remaining categories (Commentary and Problem) are comments on the progress of the story and these occurred equally in the protocols of the experts and non-experts. In order to interpret these figures we need to refer to the full transcripts.

2.2.4 Expert writers
Although the expert writers mentioned forward planning less often then the non-experts, this does not imply that the experts were poor story planners. All four writers began by setting the scene of the story by the expert writers presented an outline plot in a single verbal statement:

> Now let's say Luigi runs the restaurant and, er, he wants to create an image of, er, good image, so he wants the customers, he wants them to come back, he wants them to talk about Luigi's, so how would he do that, OK. Now let's say somebody orders wine and, er, he tastes it. OK. So, if the wine's not good they send it back. So that's no story in there. But there is a story if the wine is good and it goes back. Would be even more of a study, story, if Luigi tastes it himself and takes it back. OK. I think we've got a story. (C)

They each appeared to be guided by their outline plan throughout the sessions and referred back to it in order to verify the text: 'I'm carrying on with the dialogue now, because it's going to develop the plot' (D) – or to alter either the plan or the text in the light of discoveries made while writing: 'First I started by putting myself into the customer's situation. Then all of a sudden I realised that was totally wrong because unless the story teller was put in Luigi's plot then he would not know the story, so I made myself staff' (C). The ability to match the emerging text against the constraints (structural plans in particular) and if they diverge to revise either text or plan, appears to be a hallmark of a good writer:

> Experienced writers can pre-plan, plan and execute this plan, switching their attention from the immediate sentence to other selected focal points. (Martlew, 1983).

When generating text, the experienced writers concentrated most on the sentence level, but were able to chunk text into larger segments and to shift attention up and down levels. They 'possess a non-linear theory in which a sense of the whole writing both preceded and grows out of an examination of the parts' (Somers, 1980).

2.2.5 Young writers

Since children are less able to describe their thoughts while writing, an understanding of their writing process must come from more indirect methods, such as recordings of their activities while writing and assessments of their written drafts. Young children lack the ability of a skilled writer to create and revise plans and they appear to adopt writing strategies based on simple heuristics derived from conversation. One is the *what next* strategy (Bereiter and Scardamalia, 1982): to compose a short segment and then to reply to the mental equivalent of a conversational question ('What happened next?') by producing a link and another segment. It is not necessary that the child should consciously form a question after each segment, merely that the writing should continue *as if* the question were posed. A child cannot easily develop this strategy into a mature composing process for two reasons: firstly, because she finds it difficult to think about the structure of her text and so control it, and secondly because she is simultaneously both planning and writing individual sentences. Even if she recognises the need for higher level text structures, she may not be able to produce them, because she is attempting to consider too many levels of structure and to satisfy too many constraints at once. Only when the child becomes able to plan without writing can she lessen the mental strain of composition.

Another common writing strategy, which we shall call *limited plan,* appears to be the child's attempt to produce text to a plan (which could have been provided by a personal experience or a TV programme) while not being fully aware of its logic and structure, or unable to judge which aspects need to be communicated to the reader. This lack of awareness leads the child to create a tangled story structure containing non sequiturs or missing vital links. Such texts are discussed in more detail in Chapter 3. Again there is no simple development to mature composition. The child must first learn to view her language and her plans as entities that can be consciously shaped and revised.

2.2.6 Inexpert adult writers

So far we have suggested that maturity in writing is closely related to other cognitive skills. If this is the case then those adults who are cognitively mature, but are nevertheless poor writers, should create text by a process resembling that of experts with, perhaps, less ability to pull out elegant vocabulary or stylistic flourishes. In fact their writing, process and product, may be more like that of children:

> Poor writers, despite their maturity and different world experience, can remain as beginning writers at one or many of the component skills and levels of written language. (Martlew, 1983).

Their difficulties begin with devising a story plan. They may be aware that one is needed, but cannot produce one to suit the task: 'I haven't inspired myself by setting the scene enough to come up with a story' (Writer B). They therefore fall back on an immature coping strategy, such as 'what next' that at least allows them to generate text on any given topic, first because it can be applied to writing with no pre-specified goal and second because the writer can create content by 'acting out' the story as she writes: 'I want to involve me in the sort of atmosphere at Luigi's that I'd expect' (A); 'Now I'm going to go, so to speak, through the door of Luigi's Restaurant and see if having something to eat brings anything to mind' (B).

One method of imposing form on this strategy is to set 'milestones', incidents which must be included. Without a guiding plan to link the incidents this may present problems of continuity or lead to bizarre juxtapositions of events: 'Well first I thought of a basic structure in my head. Going to a restaurant. Getting some food. Food leading to some sort of problem, ending in mayhem, was the basic structure. Right at the beginning. But then there was how to get from step to step, as we went along' (A).

Another extension to the 'what next' strategy that can give form to a wide range of stories, is to gradually increase the tempo. This presents the problem of coordinating the pace with the time available for writing and both non-expert writers mention a difficulty with filling time. Apparently, feeling that they must keep writing and also that the story must end with a climax, they tack on further anecdotes of ever-increasing pace: 'I'm trying to extend the incident now to fill in the time. Got to extend the incident itself so need to bring more people into it' (A). 'I've got to make something happen, as I've got to keep on writing and talking for 20 minutes' (B). This exponential increase in pace is a common occurrence in children's writing. Revisions by inexpert writers are few and are confined almost exclusively to vocabulary, spelling and punctuation.

2.3 WRITING TECHNIQUES

It appears that an awareness of thought and language is a necessary but not sufficient prerequisite to becoming a skilled writer. The child or adult also needs more specific techniques for forming ideas and schemas, generating constraints appropriate to the task, taking written notes to reduce the cognitive load, proofreading to verify the text, and applying suitable transformation operators. The conscious direction of attention towards a new technique would appear to be as important to a writer as the rehearsal of a new movement is to a gymnast, allowing her to explore its applications and limitations, before incorporating it into an existing routine. Just as the overall performance of a gymnast may level out, or even decline, while she incorporates a new movement, so a writer's overall style may suffer temporarily as she acquires a new skill. Rehearsal is an important part of writing development, a time when the child needs encouragement not criticism and the opportunity to try out techniques over a wide range of topics until they become compiled knowledge and no longer a strain on conscious attention.

Bereiter and Scardamalia (1982) taught particular writing techniques to children aged 10–14, such as providing them with prompts to help them evaluate and revise each sentence in an essay. When each revision was judged separately (by an adult) the results were positive, in that changes for the better significantly exceeded changes for the worse. However, when whole essays were compared, there was no tendency for the revised version to be preferred to the originals. Bereiter and Scaradamalia state:

Our most successful experiments so far in affecting children's composing processes have not led to discernible overall improvements, as
judged by impressionistic ratings. (p. 51).

They suggest that the children were learning to write in a qualitatively different
manner:

It is *what* they are doing differently that counts, not how well they are
doing compared to how well they previously did something of a different sort. (Their emphasis.) (p. 51).

The pattern of plateaus and breakthroughs observed by Harpin and Kidder
appear to be the result of two influences. As part of normal cognitive development children bring formerly intuitive parts of the writing process into conscious
awareness, increasing their cognitive load and attenuating other skills. Later, as
they learn each new writing technique it temporarily dominates attention,
depressing overall performance until it becomes compiled and automatic. This
has important implications for the assessment of writing abilities. In order to
diagnose problems and help a child to extend her repertoire of styles and techniques we need a robust method of assessing short term qualitative changes in
children's written productions. That is the focus of the next chapter.

3

The assessment of written language

We have suggested that a child passes through stages of linguistic development, related to the Piagetian stages of cognitive development, and that these have a strong influence on a child's writing process. Returning to the two extracts given at the start of Chapter 2, how can we distinguish between them, in a way that might reveal the cognitive maturity of the two writers? We might use terms like 'vigour' and 'sensitivity' to distinguish Greene's prose, or suggest that he 'successfully evokes the childhood memories of the reader'. This method of analysis relies on the skill of a reader to interpret the author's style and intentions, then package the assessment as written criticism. Since it incorporates the experience of the reader, interpretive analysis is a useful method of literary criticism, but a poor means to understanding the writer's mind.

Another approach is to identify differences in the quantity of words or linguistic structures within the two texts. Harpin (1976) has produced six indices that 'show firm evidence of their value as measures of progress towards mature levels of language skill' (p. 59). These are:

(1) Average sentence length.
(2) Average clause length.
(3) An index of subordination (subordinate clauses as a proportion of all clauses).
(4) A weighted index of subordination (extra weight is given to a subordinate clause dependent on another subordinate clause, rather than the main clause, and to a clause containing a verbal constructions such as a participle, infinitive, or gerund).

(5) The ratio of 'uncommon' subordinate clauses to all subordinate clauses ('uncommon' here means any clause that is not an adverbial clause of time nor a noun clause acting as object).

(6) A personal pronoun index (the number of personal pronouns per 100 words).

Many other linguistic indices have been devised (Loban, 1963; Hunt, 1965; Malgady and Barcher, 1979; Golub and Frederick, 1970; Kidder, 1974). Golub and Frederick combined ten syntactic measures, similar to Harpin's, into a single index of 'syntactic density'. Kidder later added a second index of 'vocabulary intensity', measuring diversity and level of vocabulary, word building, and the use of multisyllable words, to form the most comprehensive of the quantitative linguistic measures.

Applied to the two extracts above, the 'syntactic density' index gives the Greene passage a score of 2.93, which puts it amongst writing by children of US Grade Level 4 (age 9–10), and gives Anne's extract a score of 2.61, or Grade Level 3. The vocabulary intensity scores for the two extracts were identical, equivalent to writing at seventh grade (age 12–13). Two other readability measures, Kincaid and Flesch, put Anne slightly ahead of Greene.

The quantitative measures referenced above were all derived empirically, to correlate either with the age of the writer (Hunt; Loban. Harpin) or with an expert's judgement of writing samples (Golub and Frederick; Malgady and Barcher; Kidder). They may *indicate* a child's level of writing skills relative to her peers, but they do not help to *explain* the writing process, nor a child's development of writing abilities. We require a method of text analysis that takes account of a child's cognitive and linguistic development and can indicate short-term qualitative changes in children's written language.

The relation between writing abilities and cognitive development was the central concern of a study by Britton and colleagues (Britton *et al.*, 1975) of 2212 pieces of writing by children aged 11–18. This influential piece of reasearch aimed to '[classify] writings according to the nature of the task; and, as far as possible, [find] a way of classifying that is both systematic and illuminating in the light shed on the writing process itself' (p. 3).

Drawing on work by Moffett (1968), Britton classified each piece of writing within two dimensions: the function of the writing, and its intended audience. The major function categories are 'expressive', 'poetic', and 'transactional'. Expressive is the embryonic function, seen in undeveloped children's writing and in personal or transitional adult writings, such as diary entries and rough drafts. Expressive writing 'stays close to the speaker'; to interpret it, a reader may need to understand the context in which it was written, or to share the writer's experiences.

From expressive writing emerge the poetic and transactional categories. In poetic writing, language is used as an art medium, for aesthetic appeal rather than direct communication. Transactional writing is for persuasion or conveying information. Britton subdivides this category to two further levels. The three categories are not exclusive: an advertisement, for example, may contain prose that is both poetic and transactional; a poem may be expressive and poetic.

Within the three major categories the Greene extract is transactional or trans-
actional/poetic and Anne's writing is transactional/expressive.

Britton links this method of classifying texts to the writer's emerging control of language for form and effect:

> From the area of least demand as far as the rules of [language] use are
> concerned, the learner-writer progresses by increasingly recognising
> and attempting to meet the demands of both poetic and transactional
> tasks, and by increasingly internalising forms and strategies appropriate
> to these tasks from what he reads and incorporating them into the pool
> of his resources. (Britton, 1975, p. 85).

The categories not only indicate a child's level of writing abilities, but also fit
a Piagetian explanation of writing development: a child produces expressive
writing because she cannot analyse her experiences, control her language and so
meet the needs of the task. The analysis is, however, far from complete. The
expressive category is left vague, without subdivisions. Britton uses it to signify
'undeveloped' children's writing and 'unrefined' adult text. Thus, an adult also
produces expressive writing when she is writing only for herself or is not concerned with creating a polished piece of prose or is jotting down ideas to be later
turned into a finished text. By being so diffuse, the category fails to differentiate
the particular qualities of children's writing and to reflect the turbulence that
accompanies transition to the more mature categories.

Another limitation lies in the method of assigning texts to a category:

> The process was an intuitive one, an exercise in empathy . . . It was our
> intention to employ in the categorising process the reader's more or
> less implicit awareness of the established conventions as we ordinarily
> operate them between writer and reader in our society. Only then, as
> an independent process, were the classified scripts to be submitted to
> further analysis. At this stage we hoped in particular to identify the
> linguistic features in the writing that were the vehicles for these conven-
> tions. (Had we allocated the scripts on the basis of any such features,
> we should of course have short-circuited the whole undertaking.) (p. 56).

Britton has not published a full account of the later investigation and presents it
as a research aim in *The Development of Writing Abilities (11–18)*. He suggests
that an analysis of linguistic features may lead to a greater awareness of the
criteria by which readers classify text and to an understanding of the language
resources a writer is drawing upon in a particular piece of writing.

Researchers at the Language in Education Centre at Exeter (Wilkinson
et al., 1980) are carrying out such an analysis as part of a wider investigation of
writing development. Wilkinson has devised:

> four models . . . to serve as systems of analysis — in the fields of cogni-
> tion, affect, morals and style . . . In summary they are as follows:

Cognitive. The basis of this model is a movement from an undifferentiated world, to a world organised by mind, from a world of instances to a world related by generalities and abstractions.

Affective. Development is seen as being in three movements — one towards a greater awareness of self, a second towards a greater awareness of neighbour as self, a third towards an interengagement of reality and imagination.

Moral. 'Anomy' or lawlessness gives way to 'heteronomy' or rule by fear of punishment, which in turn gives way to 'socionomy' or rule by a sense of reciprocity with others, which finally leads to the emergence of 'autonomy' or self-rule.

Stylistic. Development is seen as choices in relation to a norm of the simple literal affirmative sentence, which characterises children's early writing. Features, such as structure, cohesion, verbal competence, syntax, reader awareness, appropriateness, undergo modification. (pp. 112–113).

In applying these models to children's writing, Wilkinson discusses some linguistic features that signal types of writing style. We shall draw these into a more detailed classification of linguistic and structural features, in which the features are expressly chosen to reveal the writer's cognition. By ignoring the moral and affective aspects of writing development we are not belittling their importance; they merely lie outside the scope of our investigation.

3.1 FEATURE ANALYSIS

We begin by dividing text into three levels of structure: word and phrase; clause and sentence; section. A section is taken to be either the entire text, or a major self-contained part of it (a complete story, a chapter of this book, etc.). We shall describe features culled from a number of sources (Bereiter and Scardamalia, 1982; Halliday and Hasan, 1976; Harpin, 1976; Wilkinson et al., 1980; Sharples, 1979) that differentiate immature and mature writing at each text level. Some features, such as noun clause as sentence subject, occur more often in the writing of older children (Harpin, 1976, p. 71) but do not have an obvious connection with cognitive maturity. They have been left out of the analysis. Table 3.1 gives a summary of the features. They should be read as signposts that point, more or less accurately, towards text produced at different stages of cognitive development. The speech forms found in immature writing are indications that the child is still producing text as if for conversation. The other word and phrase level features — repetition, ambiguity, unspecific words — are all consequences of the child's inability to *decentre,* to appreciate the possible misunderstandings of a reader who does not share the writer's contextual knowledge. Signs of decentering include reflective phrases like 'I wondered whether' and abstract nouns that describe a mental state. A choice of uncommon word or phrase suggests that the writer is in control of the 'generate and select' procedure. Multiple modifiers, metaphor and simile show an ability to combine conceptual classes, and inversion — as in 'Beneath the tree lies a tiger' — indicates that the writer can detect and manipulate syntactic structures.

Table 3.1 — Features in mature and immature writing.

Features found in mature writing

Word and phrase level:	Unusual choice of word.
	Abstract nouns.
	Metaphor and simile.
	Multiple modifiers.
	Reflective commentary.
	Inversion.
Sentence level:	Cataphora.
	Ellipsis.
	Apposition.
	Coordination of sentences by complex relational words or by adverbial phrases.
Section level:	Changing levels of detail in description: 'zooming'.
	'Pyramid', 'argument' and 'process of elimination' text forms.

Features found in immature writing

Word and phrase level:	Speech idioms.
	Repetition of content words.
	Ambiguity from failure to substitute pronouns.
	Unspecific words.
Clause and Sentence level:	Coordination of sentences by 'then'.
Section level:	Arbitrary order and single level of detail in description.
	Exponential increase in pace.
	'Chain' and 'tangled' text forms.

The most common clause or sentence link of immature writers is 'then', usually a product of a 'what next' composing strategy, with the writer treating the generation of each sentence as a separate task and tacking one event onto another in a simple linear sequence. A mature writer will coordinate by expressing a relation between clauses and sentences by means of an adverbial phrase such as 'Next morning', or will vary the links to include causality, inference or contrast. Cohesive devices such as ellipsis, cataphora and apposition demand the ability to abstract syntactic patterns and to delete or substitute repeated words or structures.

As well as picking out individual linguistic features, we can study the design of an entire section. As a child gains in cognitive maturity she begins to appreciate the rules that govern her world and give it pattern and harmony. Although she may not be able to name or describe them, she learns to apply them to those activities, such as games, language, art and music, over which she has control. The rules may be implicit (a child need not cite the principles of perspective to draw a road disappearing up a hillside), but their application can be inferred from the form of the finished product.

Each text is the presentation of a network of interleaved ideas and these *associative networks* form into distinctive patterns that can reveal the cognitive structures of the writer. Associative networks were introduced by Quillian to represent the conceptual relationships between English words (Quillian, 1966) and since then we have become popular as a means of representing a wide variety of concepts, from knowledge of geography (Carbonell, 1970) to the organisation of linguistic cases (Rumelhart *et al.,* 1972). Dansereau (1978) has used associative networks to describe the structure of adult technical writing and Armbruster and Anderson (1981) have developed a similar technique, which they call 'mapping', to represent the structure of expository text. The maps have been used as part of an investigation of the comprehensibility of textbooks for children.

To analyse a text we begin by identifying the main conceptual elements and the links between each element and its neighbours. The level of detail is important: too little and regularities do not appear; too much and they are submerged. The clause is a useful starting point since it is, roughly, the realisation of a single idea and so the arrangement of clauses in a text can indicate the ordering of ideas in the mind of the writer. The clause also conveys duration, of events, and size, of objects, which, in well-constructed prose, form coherent patterns.

Clauses are the *nodes* in an associative network, linked by *arcs* that indicate the functional relationships between them. Armbruster and Anderson employ seven basic arcs in their representation of expository text – 'example'; 'property'; 'compare/contrast'; 'temporal'; 'causal'; 'enabling'; 'conditional' – plus negation and the logical connectives 'and', 'or', and 'but'. The networks below use a somewhat similar set of logical relations – 'detail'; 'compare'; 'contrast'; 'then'; 'implies'; 'cause'; 'result'; 'if/then' – with additional descriptive and temporal arcs: 'nearby'; 'contains'; 'purpose'; 'simultaneous'; 'prediction'; 'resumé'.

The sentence below is part of a story by an 11-year-old child:

|It was a playful monkey| and came down| it started throwing coconuts at me| luckily for him he missed| I picked up the coconuts| and walked away|.

The sentence splits into six clauses and Fig. 3.1 is a network showing the functional relationships between the clauses. The flow of narrative time is indicated by downward arrows and increasing levels of detail by right-pointing arrows.

A set of nodes can be grouped into a higher-level logical or rhetorical structure – comparison or problem/solution, for example – which functions as a single node in the network. On a still higher level, some texts, such as fairy stories and research reports, conform to general frameworks which prescribe an ordering of concepts to fit a convention of style or a common order of events. We shall use the term *script* to signify a topic specific grouping – 'robbery' or 'search/escape', for example – and *schema* for a more general construct, such as 'problem/solution' that can appear in a range of story settings. *Plot* will be used as a general term, to encompass both 'script' and 'schema'.

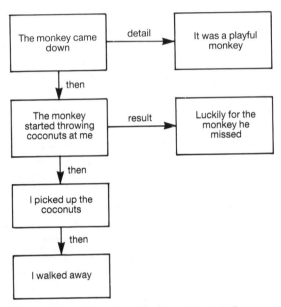

Fig. 3.1 – A network representation of part of a child's story.

Figure 3.2 shows a network representing the following sentences from a story by James, an 11-year-old child:

|I was feeling very nervous|. If I gave myself up| they'd kill me|. I thought to myself|, maybe they weren't looking| I could sneak out side|. I did just that thing|. I ran out the door| and over to my friend's house|.

The large box, incorporating a set of nodes, is a problem/solution schema, a common structure in children's narrative writing. The network need not account for every clause in the text: tautologies and virtually contentless clauses such as 'I thought to myself', can be left out without affecting the structural analysis. Conversely, elements that support the structure but do not appear in the text are included, as broken boxes, in the network. For example, 'They were not looking' is not stated explicitly, but fits the 'precondition' slot in the schema.

The pattern of conceptual dependencies in the text provides evidence as to the writer's composing strategies. A 'what next' strategy results in a *chain* story structure, consisting of a series of clauses, each describing a simple event and

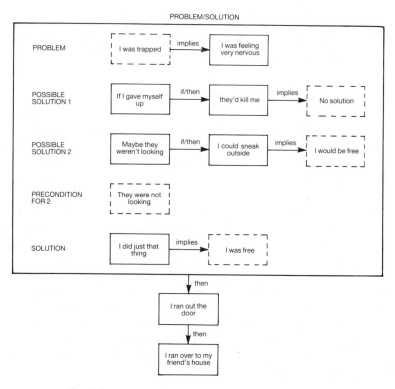

Fig. 3.2 – A network with a problem/solution schema.

linked by a temporal connective, such as 'then', 'next' or 'after that', or, in a descriptive passage, a series of objects at the same level of detail in arbitrary order. The 'limited plan' strategy produces a *tangled* story structure, with more schemas and interconnections than a chain narrative, but missing events, premises or conclusions that are vital to the plot. Another phenomenon of children's writing is an exponential increase in pace, where a sequence of clauses cover successively broader, longer events, until the pace becomes frantic and the content bizarre.

In mature writing there may be a core of narrative, but it can be broken through flashbacks and retrospection. Setting and characterisation flesh out the basic structure and sub-plots may provide parallel or embedded structures. The writer has command of rhetorical devices and alternative frameworks to the simple chain. Collins and Gentner (1981) provide some examples: *Pyramid form* (e.g. a newspaper story, in which the first sentence summarises the entire text, and then successive sections fill in more detail); *argument form* (e.g. introduction – background – definition of issues – statement of what is to be proven – arguments for and against the thesis – refutation of opposing arguments – summation); *process of elimination form* (an inverted pyramid where a writer makes an argument by successively eliminating alternatives). A mature writer may use immature features in certain circumstances, such as drafting or producing an 'expressive' piece of writing, but he is not limited to them. She has extended her linguistic range to cover other forms of language, forms that are mature and well structured, and can be varied to suit the task and audience.

3.2 METHOD OF ANALYSIS

Feature analysis can serve different needs. It can give a general measure of the maturity of a single child, or a group, or it can be a diagnostic aid, revealing particular linguistic problems, such as poor sentence coordination, and short-term variations and experiments in style. It is not so much a formal means of assessment as a way of looking at prose, as a forensic science. The text is not an end in itself, with 'right' or 'wrong' grammar, spelling and style, but a set of clues that point to the cognitive processes and structures of the writer.

The simplest method is to total up the occurrences of mature and immature features for each child. More useful for diagnosis is to count the features at each text level and also to look for an abundance of one particular feature, which may indicate a technique that the child is exploring. In the analysis of the children's essays given in Chapter 6, we have given one mark for each group of five occurrences. Thus, between one and five examples of simile in a story would score one mark, six to ten would score two, and so on. This section explains the method in more detail, with examples from essays by children aged 10–11 and is followed, in the next section, by an analysis of the two passages given at the start of Chapter 2.

3.2.1 Word level features

An unusual word is one which is clearly not in common usage by the writer's age group and for,which there is a more familiar synonym. An example would be 'turbulent' (rather than 'strong') in the phrase 'the turbulent wind'. Abstract nouns ('thought'; 'love'; etc.) are easily identifiable as are multiple modifiers (more than one adjective, or adjectival phrase modifying a noun; more than one adverb, or adverbial phrase qualifying a verb), metaphors, and smiles. Reflective commentary describes the thoughts or impressions of the author or a character, generally signalled by phrases like 'I remembered' or 'I discovered', e.g.:

> I discovered that I hadnt seen anyone on this island and decided to go
> and look for fire wood and build a fire.

Inversion is an abnormal ordering, for emphasis, of words or phrases within a clause:

> A field brightly coloured with flashing lights. Screaming is heard in
> every corner of the field. Around the Waltzers are masses of spectators
> some to frightened to go on.

Of the immature features, speech idioms need to be judged in context, since a mature writer may deliberately create a colloquial style. In the following sentence from an adventure story the clauses 'you know the people I mean' and 'there was me' are clearly drawn from verbal language:

I saw two men they seemed to be business men the were dressed in pinstripped suit and black waistcoat golden watch bowler hat umbrella and suitcase you know the people I mean and there was me with my scruffy jeans and a polo neck.

An extreme example of ambiguity arising from the overuse of pronouns is this 10-year-old child's description of a robot:

The machine couldn't move but his head could turn left and right and the board moved up and down and across the way. It had two hands with little knobs on at both of the hands and it was made of foam so it couldn't break it. It was held up by a long frame which naild into the wall.

Unspecific words are 'thing', 'some', 'someone', 'something', 'place', 'quite', 'bit' (as adverb), 'lots of', 'nice', 'got' (as in 'he got out of the room'), 'stuff' and 'went' in a context that would benefit from a more precise term:

Then I went to the rotor I went inside and then it went round and round then the floor came away and we were all sticking to the wall then I went to the dodge ums then I had no money left so I went home.

A word (or different words with the same root, e.g. 'run', 'ran' 'running') occurring three or more times in successive clauses is taken to be repetition:

Freddy is the amazing robot at Logo. He is an amazing robot because his strength is amazing.

3.2.2 Sentence level features

Halliday and Hasan (1976) describe a number of cohesive devices that a writer may use to bind together text elements across clause or sentence boundaries. Anaphora, reference back to a previous item by means of a personal pronoun, is common in verbal language and, since it demands no skills of anticipation or syntactic manipulation, is not included. Cataphora is different. Here the writer shows that she has anticipated the flow of text by inserting a forward reference: 'Look at this the star attraction the rotor'. Ellipsis achieves cohesion by the deliberate omission of a word or phrase: 'It was a playful monkey and [the monkey] came down'; 'I decided on a hill because there was a stream which I could drink from, and at the bottom [of the hill] there was trees.'.

Apposition is a means of coordinating phrases, clauses or sentences by the repetition of syntactic structures. It is sometimes difficult to distinguish from simple impoverished language. Compare 'The little man takes his boot off. He's pulling his boot over his head. He's beating his chest with his fists. He's climbing into bed' with 'Today we want to see Freddie the robot. He can pick up blocks of wood and make towers. He can do other things like pick up wooden cars and make things with wood.' The first is an extract from *Under Milk Wood* by Dylan Thomas, the second from a child's essay. For this reason we shall count only the apposition of phrases — e.g.: 'In the arcade there are bells ringing, buzzers buzzing and other unusual noises' — and of clauses or sentences that are not of a simple subject, verb, object or subject, verb, complement form. Sentence coordination by adverbial phrase — 'As I began to walk towards the stream . . .' — is counted as a mature feature, as is a relational marker of comparison (e.g. 'similarly'), adversity ('but', 'though'), contrast ('conversely', 'on the other hand'), correction ('instead', 'rather'), reason ('therefore'), result ('in consequence', 'so') and causality ('because'), e.g.: 'I decided upon the hill because there was a stream which I could drink from'. An occurrence of a simple temporal link ('then', 'next', 'after that') counts as an immature feature.

3.2.3 Section level

To build a network diagram, first split the text into its component clauses, substituting for pronouns. Thus 'The king pulled out his sword which he waved in the air.' becomes '|The king pulled out his sword.| The king waved his sword in the air.|'. Next, group together any clauses which form schemas and fill in the schema slots. Lastly, construct links between the clauses or schemas, using the following links: 'detail'; 'compare'; 'contrast'; 'then'; 'implies'; 'cause'; 'result'; 'if/then'; 'nearby'; 'contains'; 'purpose'; 'simultaneous'; 'prediction'; 'resumé' (there is no claim that these are sufficient to depict all the conceptual links in children's prose, more may need to be added). Add, as boxes bordered by dotted lines, any further nodes that are needed to complete the structure.

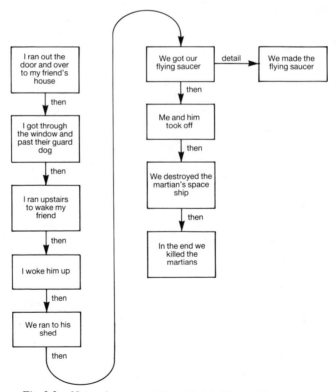

Fig. 3.3 – Network representation of a 'chain' narrative.

The network is merely a convenient illustration and the pattern will usually become clear from a reading of the text. Constructing a few sample diagrams is worthwhile, to give practice in making the mental mapping between words on a page and the underlying conceptual structure. Below are some examples of children's stories and their corresponding diagrams. Figure 3.3 represents the extract below which continues James' search and escape episode and shows a clear chain structure.

> I ran out the door and over to my friend's house. I got through the window and past there gáurd dog. Then I ran up stairs to wake my friend, then I woke him up. Then we ran to his shed and got our flying saucer that we made, then me an him, took of. Then we destroyed the martians space ship and the in the end we killed the martians. That was the end of my close encounter. Then the day after the martian's invaded earth.

The passage also shows an exponential increase in pace, a structure which usually accompanies a chain and often ends in a stock sentence, such as 'I woke up, it was all a dream'. The equivalent of a chain structure in descriptive writing is a series of objects, in no particular order, at the same level of detail (Fig. 3.4):

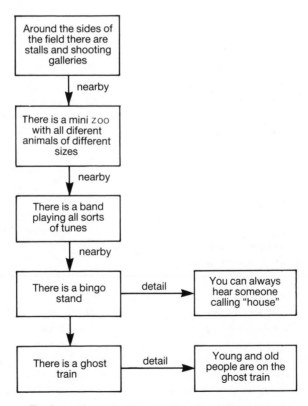

Fig. 3.4 — Network representation of a 'chain' description.

There are vans of all shapes and sizes selling ice-cream, hotdogs and hot
drinks. There are queues around all the big mechanical objects which
you can ride on.
Around the sides of the field there are stalls and shooting galleries.
There is a mini zoo with all different animals of different sizes.
There is a band playing all sorts of tunes, there is a bingo stand where
you can always hear someone calling 'house'. There is a ghost train
on which young and old people are on and seem to be enjoying there
selves.

The passage below, an entire story by an 11-year-old child, has a very different
construction:

I was on a plane flight 504 to Spain when we stopped to re fuiel. Three
men and a woman hi-jacked us and made the captain fly the plane to
Egypt. We stayd at Cairo airport for six days we didn't have mach to
eat because the hi-jackers were mean and nasty. At one time they held
the captain at gun point he said he would kill him if they didnt get
some petrol but the police said no. They shoit him and they said will
you give us some petrol the said yes but how would you drive the
plane. So they said some peopl for a captain they said the police said no
we want twenty peopl. I was one of the twenty that got free.

In just three sentences (beginning 'At one time') he weaves a complex plot
about negotiations amongst hijackers, police, and the captain of the aeroplane.
The text is so compressed, almost telegraphic, and so many crucial elements of
the plot are missing that any reconstruction must be speculative. Figure 3.5
shows an attempt to represent two of the sentences as a network, showing
the negotiations as problem-solving schemas for the hijackers and their adver-
saries. This is an extreme example of a 'tangled' story structure.

3.3 EXAMPLES OF FEATURE ANALYSIS

Figures 3.6 and 3.7 are networks for the two sample passages at the start of
Chapter 2. Table 3.2 shows the immature and mature features for each passage
and a simple count of the feature groups (one point for each group of five
features) gives a score of eight mature feature groups for Greene, and six mature
and two immature groups for Anne.

A difference in structure is evident from the layout of the two diagrams.
Anne's extract has a core of narrative, a simple chain of events, linked only by
the passage of time. The first paragraph is a description of simultaneous events,
but at the same level of detail: a view from the 'surfer'. Her final paragraph is
structurally more complex, an indication of maturity reflected at sentence level
both in the apposition 'winning money, losing money' and in the sentence
beginning 'I remembered'.

The network for Greene's passage shows no narrative, but instead a pro-
gressive 'zooming in' on detail from the tunnel down to sticks of rock. The

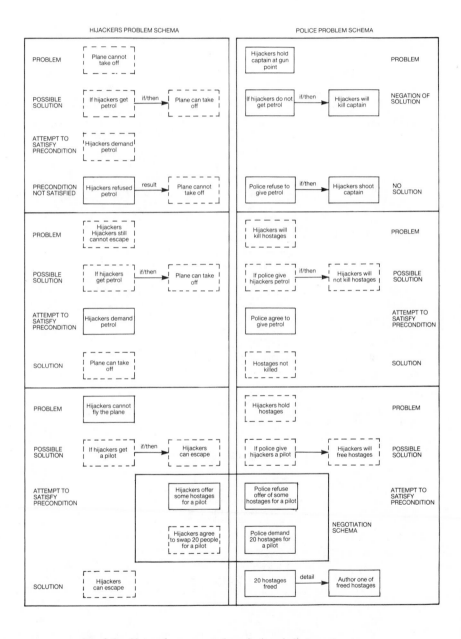

Fig. 3.5 – Network representation of a 'tangled' story structure.

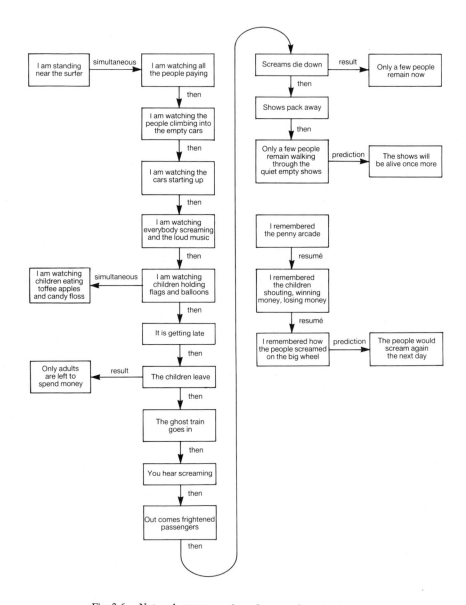

Fig. 3.6 – Network representation of extract from Anne's story.

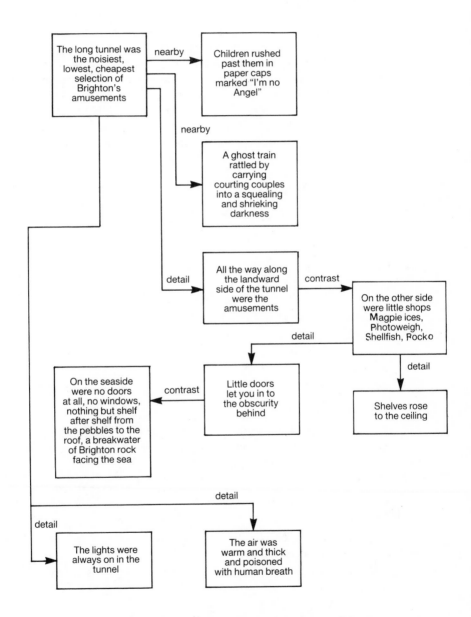

Fig. 3.7 – Network representation of the Graham Greene extract.

number of word and sentence level features show the maturity of Greene's passage. Although only one instance of apposition is recorded, all the clauses except the first are coordinated by apposition, but of a simple 'subject verb object' or 'subject verb complement' form. Anne is clearly devoting attention to sentence coordination and her first and last sentences are brave attempts at apposition and building complex subordinate clauses but, perhaps as a consequence, she fails to direct the flow of description or narrative.

Feature analysis has been successful in distinguishing between two sample passages, where quantitative indices failed. It correctly identified the one written by an immature writer and indicated that the writer appeared to be in a state of transition, producing both simple chain narrative and complex formations. Moreover, the method has a sound backing of theory: the features are direct consequences of the writer's cognitive structures and composing processes. It can indicate both a child's state of language understanding and also particular techniques that may need attention. Feature analysis is not a replacement for the impressionistic ratings of an adult reader; these are useful over longer periods

Table 3.2 – Feature analysis for two sample passages.

ANNE
Mature features

Word and Phrase Level

Multiple modifiers: 'quiet, empty'	1
Reflective commentary: 'I remembered', 'I remembered how'.	1
Inversion: 'out comes frightened passengers'.	1

Clause and Sentence Level

Ellipsis: '[I am] watching all the people', 'then [I am watching the people] climbing', '[I am watching] it starting up', '[I am watching] everybody screaming', '[I am watching] children eating toffee apples', '[I am watching] children holding flags'.	2
Apposition: 'eating toffee apples and Candy floss holding flags and balloons', 'Winning money, losing money'.	1
	—
	6

Immature Features

Clause and Sentence Level

'Then' (3 occurrences):	1

Section Level

Chain structure:	1
	—
	2

GRAHAM GREENE
Mature Features

Word and Phrase Level

Unusual words: 'rattled', 'courting', 'breakwater', 'landward'.	1
Abstract noun: 'obscurity'.	1
Metaphor: 'breakwater of Brighton rock.'	1
Multiple modifiers: 'noisiest', 'lowest', 'cheapest', 'squealing and shrieking', 'warm and thick and poisoned'.	1
Inversion: 'All the way along the landward side of the tunnel were the amusements'.	1

Clause and Sentence Level

Ellipsis: 'on the other [side were] little shops, 'obscurity behind [the shops]', 'on the sea side [of the shops]',	1
Apposition: 'no doors at all, no windows, nothing'.	1

Section Level

'Zooming' description.	1
	—
	8

Immature Features

None

---

to show that a child has successfully assimilated new skills, has been able to translate ideas into prose and has made an overall improvement in writing quality.

The associative networks are neither an exhaustive nor a canonical representation of story structure. We would not expect two readers to produce identical networks. They do, however, accommodate both simple concepts and more complex schemas. They illustrate, through diagrams that are relatively simple to construct and interpret, the logical relationships, conceptual dependencies, narrative flow, and levels of description in text. They can be aids both to planning and to interpretation of text.

4

The teaching of writing

The analysis of children's writing development in Chapter 2 has direct consequences for the teaching of creative writing. It suggests that a teaching scheme should first help a child to become aware of the language she uses and of the process of writing. Once a child has taken this major step in cognitive development, she can then be helped to build a repertoire of techniques to extend her writing abilities. This chapter describes the different approaches to teaching writing and assesses the criticisms levelled against them.

4.1 APPROACHES TO THE TEACHING OF WRITTEN ENGLISH

John Dixon, in *Growth through English* (Dixon, 1975, pp. 1–2) describes three 'models or images of English that have been widely accepted in schools on both sides of the Atlantic'. The first stresses the skills of writing and 'fitted an era when initial literacy was the prime demand'. The second encourages children to draw on the storehouse of culture and literature for their writing. The third approach provides children with opportunities to express their own experience and values through writing as a means to self discovery and 'personal growth'. They express what different groups of educators have perceived to be the prime purpose of writing:

(1) To reproduce with accuracy prescribed text forms: one's own signature: the formal letter; the report; the precis; the criticism, etc.
(2) To contribute to our cultural and literary heritage.
(3) To gain an understanding of oneself by expressing feelings, ideas and opinions in writing.

These are more ideological positions than theories of learning and, as such, they have been effective in alerting teachers to possible kinds of writing activity. However, they do tend to be mutually incompatible: lessons on Shakespeare's imagery and correct forms of address in business letters fit rather uneasily in a programme that encourages children to express needs and desires through creative writing. Schools have conventionally responded by placing each in a distinct compartment of the curriculum, hence the separate O-Level[†] examinations in Language and Literature, but this ambivalence has provoked criticism from every ideological camp and led to calls for a unified approach to the teaching of English.

Since the early 1970s, a further approach has been proposed and elaborated. This is concerned less with making value judgements about forms of writing and more with exploring the variety of language and the process of language creation. The approach fits with the analysis of children's writing development in Chapter 2 and is the teaching method used for the computer-based writing project described later in the book.

The contribution of computer science to English teaching has, so far, been negligible. So few computer programs for creative writing and language arts have been evaluated, or even described in action, that any comprehensive survey would be little more than a catalogue of software. The teaching paradigms outlined above provide a convenient framework for a survey of computers and English teaching. Rather than compiling a list of programs I shall discuss styles of software, describing a few representative programs applicable to children in the 10–15 age range and such computer-based learning projects as have been reported.

Despite the major changes in the teaching of English over the past hundred years, Britton and colleagues could still state in 1975:

> We found there were irreconcilable differences between the way writers work and the way many teachers and composition text books are constantly advising pupils to set about their tasks. (Britton *et al.*, 1975, p. 20).

The differences are due partly to the problems of putting educational research into practice. New approaches to English teaching have typically been brewed in research gatherings, such as the influential seminar on English teaching held in 1966 at Dartmouth, USA. The academic discussion has then diffused into teacher training colleges through books like Dixon's *Growth through English* (Dixon, 1975) and Government reports, particularly the Bullock Report (1975). Finally, it has percolated through to individual teachers via textbooks and teaching schemes, much diluted in the process.

But there is another, perhaps more important, reason for the poor response of schools to new ideas in English teaching: the different textbooks present contradictory and incompatible approaches.

†O-levels are public examinations taken at age 15–16 in given subjects, e.g. English language.

4.2 FORMAL SKILLS

From the Middle Ages to the late eighteenth century, the teaching of writing meant little more than ensuring that a child could copy the letters of the alphabet and produce a signature. Then, with the growing use of written language for communication and commerce, writing increased in importance, becoming one of the 'Three Rs' of Victorian education:

> The content of writing instruction was little different to that of a century before: from simple mastery of a writing instrument to copy writing and then simple dictation. In the 1870's 'composition' made its first appearance as a subject, but only for children in Standard V. This was in any case hardly as revolutionary a step as it might sound, since the pupils concerned were asked merely to write down from memory the substance of a story that had been read aloud to them. (Harpin, 1976, p. 24).

Children were taught to imitate prescribed forms of writing, from the formal letter to the literary essay, and emphasis was placed on spelling, punctuation and standard syntax. Lessons were given in sentence analysis and construction, with tasks like: 'Construct four sentences with subordinate adverbial clauses introduced by 'so that'; two to express purpose, and two to express result'.

A few schools still retain grammar exercises and a preoccupation with formal writing styles, but the main champions of the formal skills approach are now the manufacturers of computer software, who offer 'microcomputer learning laboratories' to 'teach your child the basics of English'. These are almost always 'drill and practise' programs that:

(1) Display a question.
(2) Match the student's answer against the expected response.
(3) Report success or failure.
(4) Adjust the student's score of correct answers.
(5) Repeat the process until the questions are exhausted or the student's score reaches a set limit.

The exercises may be dressed up as games with alluring sounds and pictures but the principles are the same: either a student must detect errors in spelling, punctuation or syntax, or must produce a piece of text according to a given grammatical rule.

Grammar exercises of this type have been widely criticised, for employing an obsessively didactic and rigid teaching style, for being concerned with the detection of errors rather than creativity, for pulling language out of context, and for preserving an inappropriate Latinate grammar:

> Traditional school grammars are largely contradictory and frequently absurd. Therefore children who have had problems understanding grammar have had good reason. The grammar presented to them has been frequently not understandable (Corcoran, 1970, p. 132).

Furthermore, monitoring studies have indicated no transfer of skills from grammar lessons to creative writing (Harris, 1965; Searles and Carlsen, 1960; Smith, Goodman and Meredith, 1970).

Criticism extends to the whole approach of teaching prescribed forms of writing by means of exercises separate from one another and from a context:

> Competence in language comes above all through its pursposeful use, not through the working of exercises divorced from context. Bullock, 1975, p. 528).

Over the past forty years, two movements have changed the way in which writing is taught in schools. The movements are complementary in their emphasis on the context of writing: children should be creating stories not completing grammar exercises. They differ over the place of literature in English teaching.

4.3 LITERARY APPRECIATION

A group led by F. R. Leavis proposed a curriculum bound together by literature (Leavis and Thompson, 1933; Holbrook, 1961). Literature, they argued. offers a store of experience and knowledge that children could incorporate in their own speech and writing. As important, it preserves cultural values against what was perceived to be an attack from the Philistines of mass communication:

> The case of literature is that it stands for humanity at a time when human values are not upheld . . . Among these values we number imagination, as well as the obviously acceptable ones like sympathy, understanding, and tolerance.[†]

It is difficult to see how computers might contribute to this approach, except by providing aids for writing and, possibly, access to literature. An intriguing suggestion, put forward at a conference of English teachers, is to store filmed performances of scenes from Shakespeare's plays on videodisk, along with the texts, annotations, and criticisms. A student would access the disk by computer and could watch, for example, renditions of Hamlet's soliloquy, with the spoken words displayed as subtitles on the screen. At any point the student could change to another performance of the speech. Or she could halt the film and refer to a glossary, or annotations of the text, or criticisms of the performance.

Although Thompson intended the definition of 'literature' to be wide, embracing 'quite humble work that may have no pretension to permanent value', he faced charges that children were being fed narrow elitist values:

> [The 'cultural heritage' approach] gives no cognisance to the value of the pupil's own day to day, minute by minute experience, to the validity of their own world, to their own roles as unique persons, as creative entities. (Wilkinson et al., 1980, p. 6).

4.4 'GROWTH THROUGH ENGLISH'

In 1966, teachers and academics gathered in Dartmouth, USA, to discuss the future of English teaching. From that Seminar came a new 'child-centred'

---

†Denys Thompson's address to the 1965 Conference of N.C.T.E., quoted in Allen (1980, p. 9).

approach to English teaching, promoted by Dixon in *Growth through English* (Dixon, 1975). In this approach, a child's experiences provide the content and the rationale for writing. By using all forms of language — writing; conversation; drama — a child can express, and explore, her thoughts and feelings. The teacher should provide encouragement and stimulus for imaginative writing: a pebble; a poem; a computer program. A video game can inspire a story on 'aliens'; a database program can provoke a discussion about privacy.

Harrison has devised a computer simulation program that encourages role-play (Harrison, 1983). Participants take on the roles of members of a town council and then debate the siting of a new factory. The computer displays a map of the town and accepts commands to build roads, bridges, and buildings, keeping a score of the costs and other consequences of each decision.

Other computer simulations that have been used as catalysts for discussion and writing include SLYFOX, a treasure-hunt game (Stewart, 1983) and Mission Impossible, one of many 'Adventure-type games' in which players explore an unknown territory by giving commands to the program (Chandler, 1982). Chandler has used Mission Impossible with small groups of children to inspire such language activities as code-breaking, map-making, role-play and crosswords:

> It would be no exaggeration to say that students find the game highly addictive, and the animated interaction that groups become involved in is always imaginative and cooperative (p. 81).

The 'Growth through English' approach has its own implicit set of values — the child's experience is of paramount importance and should be the focus for language activities — and from the outset it has met with criticism. Some critics lament the demotion of literature and the lack of moral guidance from teachers, who treat all forms of language as equally worthy of study. Others blame the teaching method of both the 'Growth through English' and 'literary appreciation' approach. While not denying the importance of imaginative creative writing, they believe it is insufficient as a means of improving skill in, for example, writing a report on the methods of local government, or providing a set of instructions on how to decarbonise a motorcycle (Thoulness, 1969). Even creative writing, they suggest, benefits from the learning of style and technique:

> Children reach a point where they need new techniques, having run through the satisfaction of their spontaneous performances. If the climate in one which is discouraging to such a concern there is inevitably stagnation. (Bullock, 1975, p. 164).

A few teachers have seen this as a call to 'go back to basics', to dust down the grammar books and resurrect dictation exercises. Fortunately, a new movement in English teaching offers a synthesis of imaginative personal writing and the development of language skills.

4.5 'LANGUAGE IN USE'
Halliday and Britton led a move, in the late 1960s, to apply cognitive psychology and descriptive linguistics to the teaching of English. Britton and colleagues

were mainly concerned with the writing process, the way in which a child represents meaning in language and communicates with the reader:

> When we write we are on our own. By premeditation we must arrive at the form of words which must thenceforward carry the whole of our meaning to an absent reader. What is the nature of the premeditative process by which we arrive finally at a delayed action utterance? What strategies does a writer need? (Britton *et al.*, 1966, p. 30).

Halliday's interest was the contribution of descriptive linguistics to English teaching. He argued that teaching which incorporated modern linguistic theory might be of real help in enabling children to develop their writing skills:

> The English teacher . . if he is regarded as having any responsibility for the pupil's effective mastery of the language, needs to know his underlying discipline in the same way as does any other teacher, to at least the same extent; and the relevant underlying discipline is linguistics. (Halliday, 1967).

These two strands, an understanding of children's writing process and the theoretical framework of descriptive linguistics, were woven into the *Language in Use* teaching scheme (Doughty, Pearce and Thornton, 1971):

> 'Language in Use' is concerned with the relationship between pupils and their language. This relationship has two major aspects: what pupils should know about the nature and function of language and how they can extend their command of their own language in both speaking and writing. The units aim to develop in pupils and students awareness of what language is and how it is used and, at the same time, to extend their competence in handling the language. (p. 8–9).

The scheme promotes an 'ecological' approach to English teaching. Students examine language in a variety of contexts – a weather forecast, a newspaper advertisement, a police interview, etc. – to gain an understanding of its function and application. They are then asked to write their own examples of the language mode and register being studied. For example, they might write a newspaper article about an unusual hobby, or produce an episode of a radio play in regional dialect. The emphasis is on extending a child's range of language. Linguistics is brought in to describe the possibilities of language, not prescribe particular forms.

When the scheme was published in 1971, it was received with some enthusiasm. The Bullock Report, the major British Government investigation of English teaching in school, devotes a page to *Language in Use* and, while admitting the danger that 'unimaginatively used, the programme can become divorced from other aspects of English teaching' (Bullock, 1971, p. 175), it concludes that:

> Mediated by a teacher who can turn practical suggestion into imaginative reality, work of this kind has a valuable contribution to make. (p. 175).

Valuable though it is, *Language in Use* has never gained wide acceptance in the classroom and in recent years has attracted criticism both for its approach and its structure. Bullock (p. 175) reports a judgement of some teachers that *Language in Use* 'does not commit itself to fundamental values, that it remains a training in techniques', an echo of an address given by Inglis to the 1971 Conference of NATE (Allen, 1980, p. 57). Doughty and his colleagues never claim, however, to provide a course in literary appreciation, nor to develop a child's powers of taste and discrimination. Whether or not to teach cultural and literary values is still the subject of much debate. The authors have opted to avoid the issue by teaching language usage, leaving value judgements to the child and teacher.

Another, more pragmatic, limitation of *Language in Use,* one shared by other linguistics textbooks, is the lack of aids for language manipulation. In one section, students are encouraged to examine errors caused by the misapplication of grammatical rules, for example:

These shoes hurt my foots.
She's taked my clothes.

The exercise would be much enhanced by a simple means of generating sentences to reveal a rule of grammar and its exceptions. Thus, a pupil might suggest a rule for past tense such as 'verb+ed' and be offered:

She's mended my clothes.
She's finded my clothes.
She's sewed my clothes.
She's washed my clothes. (etc.)

Another section asks the students to rewrite an article from a 'specialist' magazine without using technical language. Here they require a method of revising sections of text, without either producing a jumble of insertions and deletions or rewriting the entire passage. A set of aids for language understanding and text manipulation would provide a test-bench for the experiments proposed in *Language in Use*.

The two examples above indicate a need for two types of language aids: a system to model language, so that children could create and explore linguistic structures, and writing aids that can help a child to plan, compose, and revise text. Some computer programs of both types are described below. None has been evaluated with large groups of children, so any evidence of their value rests on formative evaluation, or on anecdotes and assertions by those who developed the programs.

4.5.1 Models of language
A tenet of artificial intelligence research is that models can be valuable learning aids. A good way to understand the laws, constraints, and possibilities of a complex rule-governed system is to build models of the system, subject to the same rules, and then perform experiments on them. This methodology can be as useful in the school as in the research laboratory. Howe suggests that a child

can learn to understand and control a complex mechanism through the problem solving process involved in constructing and testing models of the system (Howe, 1979):

> To promote real understanding of mechanisms, there is a need for a modelling system which allows a child to be creative. It should provide her with an opportunity to alter pre-determined models and even to create her very own models.

A child with a Meccano set (Erectorset in the USA), who builds a bridge, runs a toy car over it, notices that the bridge sags, and so strengthens it with a triangular brace, is carrying out this process of building and testing models.

The model need not be a physical one; the prime requirement is that it should build on terms and concepts that are familiar to the child. Turtle geometry is the best known computer-based modelling system for children. The child extends his intuitive understanding of shape, space and direction by commanding a 'turtle' (a small motorised cart with a pen attached) to draw geometric shapes. The models she creates are programs (Fig. 4.1) that can be tested by running them and comparing the results with her predictions. *Turtle Geometry* by Abelson and Di Sessa (1981) is a full and fascinating account of this procedural approach to mathematics.

Computer-based modelling aids have been developed for a variety of school mathematics topics (de Boulay, 1978; Howe *et al.*, 1979) as well as composing tunes (Bamberger, 1972), orbital mechanics (Di Sessa, 1975), and simple electrical circuits (Borning, 1979). Gains in mathematical ability through modelling

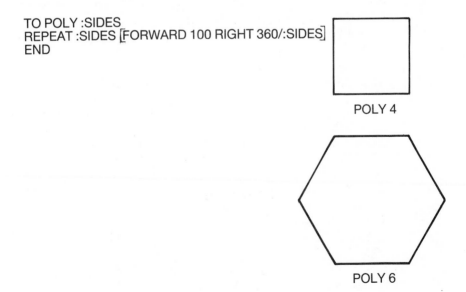

```
TO POLY :SIDES
REPEAT :SIDES [FORWARD 100 RIGHT 360/:SIDES]
END
```

POLY 4

POLY 6

Fig. 4.1 — A Logo program.

in Logo have been reported by Milner (1973), Howe and O'Shea (1978), du Boulay (1978) and Finlayson (1985).

Over the past decade computer programs have been developed to model many aspects of language production and comprehension — generative grammars, parsers, translation systems, information retrieval systems — and some of these programs are now being adapted for use by children. They offer an environment in which children can create grammars, look for patterns in language, manipulate text systematically by applying rules of transformation, and explore the linguistic constraints of meaning and syntax. In Chapter 2, it was suggested that a child needs to create and manipulate language structures at all textual levels, from the word to the section, so the computer-based modelling aids will be described within this dimension, starting at word and phrase level.

Johns (1983) has devised two programs for word manipulation on the Sinclair ZX81 microcomputer: 'A/AN' and 'S-ENDING'. A/AN is a simple pattern recogniser that places the correct form of indefinite article before a noun phrase typed in by the user. If, for example, the user types 'uniformed person' it replies 'a uniformed person'; given 'uninformed person' it replies 'an un-informed person'. S-ENDING carries out a similar process for plurals. Both programs allow a child to infer the rules of word and phrase formation and so learn that language contains regular patterns.

A number of educational programs have been written to manipulate language at the sentence level. Iliad (Bates and Wilson, 1981) was developed by Bates and colleagues for a mainframe computer and reprogrammed in Pascal for the Apple microcomputer. It contains rules to generate many different transformations of a given sentence. For example, from the sentence 'John ate the apple' it can produce:

Did John eat the apple?
What did John eat?
Who ate the apple?
What did John do to the apple?
He ate it.

These rules are embedded in a tutorial program, aimed at deaf children who have difficulties in mastering such language forms as negation, question forma-tion, and sentences containing complex verb phrases. The tutorials are presented as question and answer drills, reminiscent of traditional grammar lessons, com-plete with cheerfully patronising replies to correct answers. In the extract below, the words typed by the student are in bold type. When a student types a partly-correct reply, the program repeats the correct portion ('What did Jane' below). If the student still cannot work out the answer, she can type a '#' and the pro-gram will supply a further word ('What did Jane write').

1. The adults bought Mrs. Brown a dog.
Make a WH-question about the object.
> **What did the adults buy Mrs. Brown?**
A worthy effort, Lyn!

2. Jane wrote Andi a letter.
> **hint**
Type in a WH-question.
> **What did Jane wrote Andi?**
> What did Jane #
> What did Jane write **Andi**
I couldn't have done it better myself!

Stripped of its teaching component, Iliad is a powerful sentence generator based on a transformational grammar:

> The sentence generator possesses detailed knowledge of the syntactic structures of each sentence it produces. For example, it maintains a record of the part of speech (noun, verb, determiner, etc.), it notes the tense of each clause, and it is capable of determining the grammatical relations born by different constituents; for example, which noun in a sentence is its subject, direct object, or indirect object. In transformational terms, Iliad produces phrase structure trees for both the deep and surface structures of each sentence. (Bates and Wilson, 1981, pp. 5–6).

The report on Iliad mentions a debugging environment for the program called the 'syntactic playground' in which the user can develop and test various components of the generator. It allows a system programmer or linguist to have complete control over all aspects of the generation process, testing syntactic hypotheses and exploring the power of the language generator. If this 'syntactic playground' could be adapted for use by children, it would come far closer to the aims of *Language in Use* than Iliad's restricted grammar drills.

An early example of language tools for children was a context-free grammar and pattern-matching parser, written in Logo by Kahn (1975). The parser consists of Logo procedures to match specified word patterns, with '$' standing for any series of words and '?' representing a 'variable. Thus, the pattern [$ NAME IS ?NAME $] will match word strings like 'I THINK YOUR NAME IS JOHN' or 'YOUR NAME IS ALEX, I BELIEVE' and output the word corresponding to ?NAME - 'John' or 'Alex' in the examples above. A child can specify syntax patterns to match different sentence structures.

With the context-free grammar procedures, a child can specify a grammar to the computer and then use it to generate sentences. Kahn reports a pilot project with a single child, aged 13, and concludes that the child 'seemed to pick up quickly the writing of generation rules and patterns for parsing' (Kahn, 1975, p. 18).

Kahn's sentence generator is similar in design to the POEM programs, also written in Logo (Sharples, 1978). They are the forerunners of the programs described in chapter five and were used by three boys, aged 15. The aim of the project was to provide the boys with the means to generate 'poems'. They began with POEM1, which generates random strings of words. They then classified the words according to part of speech and gave them as input to POEM2.

This program generates word strings to follow a syntactic pattern. Given the pattern 'ARTICLE ADJECTIVE NOUN VERB ARTICLE NOUN' and the following vocabulary:

ARTICLE: a, the
NOUN: mouse, cat, lion
ADJECTIVE: big, tiny
VERB: eats, devours

It might generate, 'a tiny cat devours the mouse' or 'a big lion eats the lion'. The children produced a number of syntax patterns, including one to generate a Christmas poem:

XMAS

THE PRESENT SPARKLES
THE SONG SHINES
HARK XMAS
AND THE HEAVENLY TREE GLOWS SWEETLY NEAR THE DECOR-
   ATION
HARK THE GORGEOUS BELL.

The next program, POEM3, generates word strings that 'make sense'. The program must first be provided with a vocabulary. Each word in the vocabulary is given a part of speech and a set of 'meanings', which define its semantic features, for example: NEWWORDS "NOUN [SNOWBALL] [THING AIR MOVING]. A syntax pattern as for POEM2, is then given to the program and it generates strings of words that are matched for meaning as well as ordered by the syntax pattern. The children created vocabularies and patterns for thematic poems, for example:

DRY PATH

LONELY MOON FADES SUBTLY
IN COLD PLAINS
BLACK CLOUDS
FROST FADES BY WISH

WE FEED SLOWLY

BLACK PATH FADES TO RED ROCKS
I FEED

Towards the end of the project, the children were given tape-recorded interviews. These indicate that they were able to name parts of speech and discuss sentence structure. Just as important, they enjoyed the experience of creating computer poems and fulfilled their own objectives. At the start of the project, one of the children had remarked 'If the poems are good enough we could get them published in the school magazine'. They submitted the best of the poems produced during the project and three were accepted for publication. Another program for generating poems is Compupoem by Stephen Marcus (Marcus, 1981). It prompts the user for various parts of speech and then forms these into a poem. A later version also offers advice on parts of speech, on choosing various kinds of words, and on 'zen and the art of computer poems'.

The 'Storymaker' developed by Rubin (1980) for the **Apple II** computer, allows a child to create and manipulate larger units of text than the sentence, in order to develop her skills of story planning. Alternative story structures are represented as a *tree* composed of *nodes* connected by *branches*. Each node contains a *story segment* (a sentence or paragraph of text) and one or more branches may emanate from each node, representing alternative continuations of the text. A single path from the *root node* (the first sentence or paragraph of the story) to a *leaf node* (one of the many alternative last sentences or paragraphs) constitutes a complete story. A part of a story tree used by Storymaker is shown in Fig. 4.2.

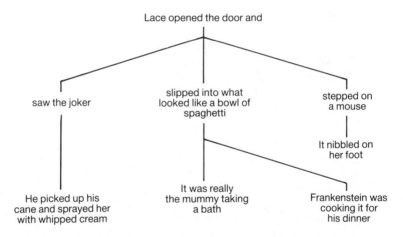

Fig. 4.2 – Part of a tree from the Storymaker program.

The child first creates a story by chosing one branch at each node. As the child selects a branch the program adds its segment of text to the story on the screen and displays the next set of alternative segments. Rubin reports:

> Children who used the 'Storymaker' learned that their early choices had definite, sometimes surprising consequences. This fact made 'Storymaker' an excellent tool for demonstrating the structure and coherence of stories. (Zacchei, 1982).

The child may either explore story pathways by making choices based on personal preference or work towards a goal generated by the program. This goal describes something that will occur during the story – an event, a character, a final outcome. If the child's version of the story does not match the expected version then a response such as 'I'm sorry, but your story is not exactly the one I expected' is given.

A version of the program, called 'Storymaker Maker', allows a child to create and modify her own story structures. While exploring a story tree the child may choose, at any node, to create new branches and compose and type in segments to continue the story. Rubin suggests that the activity of exploring and creating alternative story structures develops skills which are difficult to exercise: problem solving and reasoning, evaluation and inference.

> More significantly, the child uses skills to extract meaning, applying knowledge about story structure and progression to a specific set of story segments. (Rubin, 1980).

It is important to note that, in the Storymaker programs, the content of the stories is not the main stimulus to learning; the child learns by understanding and manipulating the model (in this case story structures) represented in the program and by discussing her experiences with a teacher or peers.

4.5.2 Writing aids

Storymaker Maker is as much a writing aid as a language modelling program; it is a means for children to create and combine possible stories. Computer-based writing aids can offer assistance to a writer, or replace pen and paper as the writing medium. They range from simple word processors to tutorial systems giving advice on spelling, punctuation, and style.

Most microcomputer manufacturers offer word processing packages as standard software. Some schools have made these available to students but, given the shortage of machines in schools, there is generally no possibility of providing a computer for each child. One school, Heaton school in Newcastle, has been fortunate in borrowing Microwriters for use in creative writing projects. The Microwriter is a small hand-held computer terminal with a 14-character display, a memory that holds four pages of A4 text, and limited word processing capabilities. It can be connected to a VDU for a full-screen display, or to a printer. In an imaginative creative writing project, 27 children aged 13–14 were taken to an industrial museum and asked to record their impressions and ideas. They used the Microwriters as notepads and then, back at school, they expanded and revised the notes into reports (Clark, 1983).

Levin and colleagues at the University of California, San Diego have produced a program called the 'Writer's Assistant' (Levin, Boruta and Vasconcellos, 1982) in Pascal for the Apple microcomputer. It is based on the Pascal Text Editor, with additional commands that allow a child to check spelling, to experiment with word combinations and to merge sentences into a paragraph. The program has been tried out with children aged 9–10 who used it to create a classroom newspaper. They typed text to the computer, revised it by adding, deleting and rearranging words, phrases and lines of text and then printing out a final copy. The newspaper text file was structured into different sections (news, sports, TV reviews, cookbook, jokes, etc.) and the children worked on one issue of the newspaper per month.

Levin reports a preliminary evaluation, in which children in the experimental class and in a control class wrote on a topic using pencil and paper. The essays were written at the start and finish of a four-month experimental period, during which time the experimental group children used the Writer's Assistant. Levin does not report the number of hours that this group spent at the computer, nor the comparative activities of the control group. The essays were analysed for length and overall quality (with organisation and adherence to topic emphasised) by a judge blind to the classroom from which the samples belonged. Levin reports significant increases in both measures for the experimental group and no overall increase for the control group.

Newsdesk, published by Cambridge Language Arts Software, puts word processing in the context of a newspaper office. The child is given background information to a news story and, as she types in her copy, the program displays further news items on a 'teleprinter' line at the bottom of the screen.

A richer writing environment is provided by the 'Quill' programs, developed by Bolt, Baranek and Newman Inc. for the Apple II computer (Collins *et al.,* 1982). The five programs comprise a child's text editor, a publication system which enables children to design printed newspapers, an electronic mail system, an information exchange in the form of an indexed database and an activity kit with language games and activities.

The 'Writer's Workbench' is a growing collection of programs developed by Bell Labs. for use with minicomputers on the UNIX operating system. They are designed to aid a writer in evaluating and modifying text:

> The programs that evaluate surface features [of text] check for possible spelling errors, consistency of usage and general punctuation errors. The more complex language analysis [program] provide information on the overall readability of the text as well as sentence complexity . . . Passive sentences, which may add to the difficulty of reading a text, are highlighted by the program. Awkward or wordy phrases are indicated by another program that also provides alternative phrases for substitution. Other Writer's Workbench programs include a syllable counter, a simple re-formatter that puts imperative sentences in a numbered list, and a program that assigns a part of speech to each word in a sentence. (Frase, 1980).

A similar system is EPISTLE, developed at IBM (Miller, Heidorn and Jensen, 1981), which detects several classes of grammatical error in a text, for example disagreement in number between the subject and verb.

Although the Writer's Workbench and EPISTLE make disputable judgements about grammar and style, a writer retains control over the text and makes the decisions on whether to accept or reject the changes. Programs that interrupt a writer to offer spelling corrections or advice on style may pass over the line between helpful assistance and unwarranted intervention. Where this line is drawn depends on the type and quality of advice, the nature of the task, and the proficiency of the writer. An adaptive writing aid might contain representational models of the writer and text which it could consult to decide whether or not to interrupt the writer with advice. No such system has yet been implemented, but the two programs described below were designed to provide information about different levels of intervention.

The CAC program has been designed by Woodruff *et al.* (1981) and implemented in Basic on a 32K Commodore PET microcomputer. The program operates at the sentence/paragrpah level and offers children advice on composing persuasive text. It uses a technique the authors call 'procedural facilitation' in which a child is helped to make better use of her latent knowledge by having a computer program (or trained adult) lessen the executive burden of mental tasks, so freeing the child to carry out kinds of information processing that would normally exceed her capabilities.

The child begins a session with CAC by typing text into the computer, with the program acting as a simple word processor. If, however, the child presses a 'help' key, or the terminal is inactive for more than 20 seconds, then the program prompts: 'May I help you?'. When the answer is 'yes' it presents a *help menu* and the child can choose to take advice on, for example, 'following an argument plan' or 'producing the next sentence'. The guidance offered by CAC is based on the text most recently composed by the child. If a child asks for advice on producing the next sentence then the program searches the last complete sentence for a *keyword* such as 'believe', 'reason' or 'example'. On finding the word 'reason', for example, the computer would print 'Let's say more about your reasons so the reader will understand'. The prompt is determined by the first keyword found.

The program will not interfere by offering help unless requested by the child, and the authors report that children (grade 6 elementary school) were 'willing and able to work interactively with the computer while composing and enjoyed the experience'. Essays produced with the aid of the computer, however, were not significantly different, when rated for overall quality, from those written with pencil and paper.

A second program CAC2 was designed, which provides more active intervention, presenting a question such as 'Do you have an opinion on this topic?' or 'Have you mentioned any facts to support you reason' after each sentence typed by the child. Each question is determined by the child's response to previous questions and they are intended to emulate those an expert writer might ask himself while composing.

Thirty-six children (grade 8) were set a persuasive writing topic and assigned to one of three groups. The first group wrote using pencil and paper, the second composed with the CAC2 program and the third used CACB, a program that acted simply as a typewriter, with no prompts or advice.

The essays were rated on an eight-point scale for persuasiveness and clarity of argument and the authors report that 'overall CAC2 papers were given lower rates than CACB papers'. When the children were asked to rank, from hardest to easiest, the difficulty of condition to write under, the pencil and paper was ranked as hardest, CACB as the second and CAC2 as the easiest. The authors offer an explanation (based on further questioning of the children) that:

> the program was having an effect on students' choices of what to say
> . . . The program may have been setting in motion a new composing
> strategy — a more sophisticated strategy, but one which students could
> not use to their advantage at the first attempt.

The authors are undecided about the best level of computer intervention and suggest two strategies for investigation: to develop more powerful techniques of procedural facilitation and to allow children to control the amount of computer assistance, or to develop more sophisticated response-sensitive questions and allow the computer to guide the learner from the beginning to the end of the composing process.

4.6 TEACHING SCHEME

Computer-based aids for writing and language exploration can fill a gap in the *Language in Use* approach to English teaching, providing children with the means to explore and manipulate language. A lack of tools is not the only limitation of *Language in Use*. It also 'lacks any real structure to the teacher unversed in linguistic knowledge' (Brown, 1975). It is designed as a broad teacher's guide, rather than a textbook and 'a number of teachers have expressed perplexity as to how *Language in Use* should be used. Part of the difficulty is . . . the fruitless search for teacher-proof material' (Muir, 1975). A teacher-proof scheme must provide more explanation and guidance than *Language in Use* while still leaving room for interpretation.

5

Computer models of mind

The computer is a marvellous modelling kit. Any child who has enjoyed the challenge of Meccano, Lego or building blocks, should be captivated by computers. Computers are especially suited to constructing models of the mind. Artificial Intelligence programming languages, such as LISP, PROLOG and POP, have been designed for just this purpose, providing a workbench for testing theories of human cognition and for exploring mental processes. The challenge for educationalists is to adapt these for use by children, aligning them with a child's mind, reasoning and view of the world, without sacrificing their power and flexibility. Logo, a derivative of LISP, was the first attempt at a general purpose modelling language for children and has been deservedly successful. The operators and data structures of LISP are too low-level for children (the equivalent of giving a young child a log and saw and suggesting that she construct some wooden building blocks), so turtle graphics was added to Logo to give the child a high-level modelling kit (or *microworld*) for exploring geometry.

This chapter describes a similar kit for language. Just as turtle geometry has been added on to other programming languages, so the language kit has seen a number of incarnations. The first parts were written in Logo as part of the Poetry from Logo project outlined in Chapter 4. These were rewritten in POP-2 (an artificial intelligence programming language) and extended for the teaching scheme to be described in Chapter 6. Since then, versions of the Phrasebooks and Boxes programs have appeared in Logo for the Apple II and BBC B micros. Appendix 1 contains Logo listings of Phrasebooks and Boxes, plus a version of the NETTY program.

For consistency, I have chosen to describe all the progams here in terms of Logo as it is both an appropriate and widely known language, even though the

WALTER text editor and a full version of the PAT text generator currently only exist in POP-2. At the time of writing, faster and more extensive versions of Logo are becoming available for 16-bit microcomputers and these would be suitable hosts for the larger programs.

5.1 DESIGN CRITERIA

There are a number of design criteria that need to be satisfied in order to build a large user-friendly modelling kit. The kit must be:

Familiar   A child with no knowledge of programming should be able to carry out worthwhile experiments using familiar terms. It should build on a child's existing awareness of thought and language.

Accessible The child should be given a concrete device that reveals the important aspects of the system being modelled. (In turtle geometry the turtle serves that purpose.)

Helpful   The computer should offer comprehensible error messages and on-line help.

Useful   The child should be able to represent and solve interesting problems.

Extensible As the child learns new techniques for manipulating language, she should be able to incorporate them in the kit, so that it always reflects her current level of understanding.

Layered   There should be distinct layers of operation, with the deeper ones requiring more skill but allowing a wider range of explorations.

The language toolkit described here has three layers of operation. At the top level, the user is guided through each activity by captions and prompts for input. At the next, she has direct access to the language structures and operations, and can incorporate them in new programs. At the lowest level is the implementation language, in this case Logo, and the procedures that drive the toolkit. The kit models the writing processes of Generate and Select, Verify and Transform and Select, operating on data structures that are analogous to mental concepts. The child starts on familiar ground – generating random words, writing and editing a story, and playing an 'Adventure' game – but as she progresses, the child pushes into new areas of language and thought. In order to generate more realistic sentences and poems, to make more general alterations to the story, or to extend the Adventure game, she needs to know about the grouping of words into categories, the constraints of structure and meaning on text, the patterns of language and the organisation of objects in space and time.

The kit consists of three programs, named PAT (PATtern generator), WALTER (Word ALTERer) and NETTY (NETwork TYpes).

5.2 PAT

PAT is a means of exploring the patterns and constraints of language. The child's goal is to 'teach' the computer to write English, by first commanding the program to generate words at random and then specifying a series of grammars to generate increasingly refined phrases, sentences and poems. The program is no substitute for the creative act of writing, any more than turtle geometry is a substitute for creative drawing; it is designed to help a child to appreciate the regularities in language. There are three basic commands, 'put', 'sort' and 'do'. 'Put' adds words or phrases to a 'grammar box', the simplest of which is just a box of words (commands and data typed by the user are in bold):

? **put**

BOX NAME: **word**

ITEM: **cat**
ITEM: **sleeps**
ITEM: **the**
ITEM: **softly**
ITEM: **fades**
ITEM: **leaps**
ITEM: <Pressing the 'return' key without entering a word ends the program>

WORD

cat
sleeps
the
softly
fades
leaps

DO takes a word out of the box, at random, each time the box name appears in the 'word pattern'. An ampersand indicates a new line of words:

? **do**
WORD PATTERN: **word word word & word word word**

Softly cat the
leaps softly fades

The PAT program recognises upper or lower case letters and automatically inserts a capital letter at the start of the output and after a full stop. The next stage is to sort the words into different boxes. The child may choose the classification method and miss out any word with no obvious place:

? **sort**

BOX NAME:**word**
    cat
NEW BOX NAME: **animal**
    sleeps
NEW BOX NAME: **doing**
    the

NEW BOX NAME: <Child leaves 'the' unsorted>
    softly
NEW BOX NAME: **how**
    fades
NEW BOX NAME: **doing**
    leaps
NEW BOX NAME: **doing**

ANIMAL

cat

DOING

sleeps
fades
leaps

HOW

softly

The word pattern can now contain a mixture of box names and their order determines the finished sentence:

  ? **do**

WORD PATTERN: **The animal doing how**
The cat sleeps softly

WORD PATTERN: **The animal doing the animal**
The cat fades the cat

At this point the child could be introduced to grammars and parts of speech as a means of creating better and more interesting word patterns. Suppose a child wants the computer to generate 'haiku', a simple form of poetry developed in ancient Japan. She faces a number of challenges. She needs to: read existing haiku poems to discover their intentions, subject matter, rhythms and patterns; abstract those aspects of haiku that could be 'taught' to PAT; write a 'grammar' to generate sample poems; compare PAT's versions with human-written haiku; refine the grammar to improve the poems.

The child will discover that haiku poems are about nature and its seasons. They do not rhyme and contain three lines with a total of seventeen syllables. An example of human-written haiku (from McDougall, Adams and Adams) is:

Late cold showers fall.
Tiny blossoms open and
Greet the new warm sun.

If we ignore the restriction of seventeen syllables, then it is not difficult to write a word pattern for the poem:

  adjective adjective noun verb.
  adjective noun verb conjuction
  verb article adjective adjective noun.

We now need a suitable vocabulary

BOX	CONTENTS
adjective:	still, lifeless, fragile, white, hungry
noun:	Petal, bird, flower, snowflake, rock
verb:	stands, greets, falls, soars, welcomes, sings
conjunction:	and, then
article:	a, the

Given this pattern and vocabulary PAT might generate:

Hungry lifeless bird falls.
White rock greets then
waits a still still petal.

The last two verbs are clearly inappropriate, yet swapped around would make better sense. The child might ponder on the difference between 'waits' and 'greets' and then sort the box of verbs into two further boxes, according to whether or not the verb may be followed by a noun:

? **sort**

BOX NAME: **verb**
stands
NEW BOX NAME: **verb1**
greets
NEW BOX NAME: **verb2**
falls
NEW BOX NAME: **verb1**
soars
NEW BOX NAME: **verb1**
welcomes

NEW BOX NAME: **verb2**
sings
NEW BOX NAME: **verb1**

The next problem concerns plurals. In the original poem the first two nouns are plural. The phrase 'bird falls' in the PAT poem is singular and appears strange because there is no article ('a' or 'the') before it. The child could create new boxes called 'pluralnoun' and 'pluralverb', but that would require entering each noun and verb twice. It is simpler to state that a plural noun is a singular one followed by 's', and a plural verb is a singular verb with 's' removed (leaving aside the problem of words with irregular endings). This means creating boxes containing not words, but the names of other boxes:

? **put**

BOX NAME: **pluralnoun**

ITEM: **noun+s**

ITEM:

? **put**

BOX NAME: **pluralverb1**

ITEM: **verb1−s**

ITEM:

? **put**

BOX NAME: **pluralverb2**

ITEM: **verb2−s**

ITEM:

Now whenever 'pluralnoun' is found in a word pattern, then 'noun+s' is generated, but 'noun' is the name of a box, so a word is chosen from it, e.g. 'petal'. The '+s' indicates that 's' will be added to the end of the word, this 'petals'. The same occurs for verbs, except that the final 's' is removed. The word pattern for haiku is now rewritten for the new box names:

? **put**

BOX NAME: **haiku2**

ITEM: **adjective adjective pluralnoun pluralverb1 & adjective
pluralnoun pluralverb1 conjunction & pluralverb2 article
adjective adjective noun.**

ITEM:

? **do**

WORD PATTERN: **haiku2**

Fragile lifeless rocks stand.
Still petals sing and
Greet a white still bird.

PAT is an implementation of a powerful linguistic tool: a context-free grammar. The same set of word boxes can serve to generate many different types of sentence:

BOX	CONTENTS
sentence:	nounphrase verb
	nounphrase verb2 nounphrase
nounphrase:	article adjective noun
	article noun

With these boxes and those already created for the haiku, a word pattern of 'sentence. sentence.' might generate:

The bird greets the fragile rock. The flower sings.
or
A lifeless petal stands. The still rock welcomes a white rock.

No prescribed grammar of English is concealed in the program; the child is free to determine the name and contents of each box, and so of course may classify a word wrongly or specify a bizarre word pattern. Ten-year-old children are, however, well able to recognise sentences with deviant grammar, so any discrepancies between the child's intentions and the performance of the program can give a child valuable feedback on the limitations of her understanding. The emphasis of learning is on adequacy rather than correctness. If a child generates the sentence 'The angry chases the fierce dog.' then the source of the problem is clearly around the word 'angry' and an inspection of the boxes will show either that the word has been wrongly classified or that the sentence pattern is inadequate and needs to be improved.

However carefully the patterns and boxes are chosen, the generated text still lacks a vital ingredient: agreement of meaning. An extension to PAT combines the context free grammar with 'semantic markers' (Katz and Fodor, 1963). Each word in a box can be given one or more markers, for example:

BOX	CONTENTS	MARKERS
noun	rock	inanimate, still, ground
	bird	animal, moving, air
	snowflake	inanimate, cold, moving, air

The pattern indicates the particular words that must agree in meaning:

BOX	CONTENTS	MARKERS
nounphrase	the adjective #1 noun #1	

Thus the noun agrees in meaning with the adjective in a nounphrase. The blank under the 'markers' column indicates that nounphrases have no overall meaning. PAT provides simple prompts for adding markers to the words in each box and the three poems below were produced by one grammar of some thirty word boxes and a vocabulary of around 200 words.

A lonely boy.

Wait!
A boy still hates you
Weep beside a stream.

A calm glass.

I think
I am like the glass.
I forget quickly.

Why does my waiting child like to talk?
Why does my girl wish to dream of my song?
You are like a song.
By herself my waiting girl dreams.

5.3 WALTER

Another aspect of language use is text editing and transformation and WALTER is a syntax-directed text editor. At its simplest it acts as a three command word processor. The command 'new' is used to create text, 'show' to highlight specified word patterns, and 'change' to transform the text. Unlike conventional word processors it can follow rules for sentence-level text transformations. It is best described by an annotated dialogue (WALTER overwrites the screen to highlight each transformation in turn. Since this would take up too much space on the printed page, only the final state of the screen is shown in the examples below).

? **new**   <The child types a new story to WALTER>
STORY: **Once there was a pretty princess. The**
STORY: **princess lived in a big house in a**
STORY: **a forest. The forest was drak. She was**
STORY: **lonely because she had no friends to**
STORY: **play with in the house.**
STORY:

? **change**   <Alter the text>

OLD WORDS: **drak**
NEW WORDS: **dark**

<Correct the spelling. The
first occurrence of the
misspelling is highlighted
and the child presses a YES
button to make the
alteration. The cursor moves
to the next misspelling and
so on to the end of the text.>

Once there was a pretty princess. The princess
lived in a big house in a a forest. The forest
was dark. She was lonely because she had no
friends to play with in the house.

? **show**   <Highlight a word pattern,
in this case every noun in the
passage.>

WORD PATTERN: **noun**

Once there was a pretty **princess**. The **princess**
lived in a big **house** in a **forest**. The **forest** was
dark. She was lonely because she had no **friends**
to play with.

? **change**

OLD WORDS: **house**   <As each change is highlighted
NEW WORDS: **castle**   the child either presses YES
                                   to accept it or NO to reject it.>

Once there was a pretty princess. The princess
lived in a big castle in a a forest. The forest was
dark. She was lonely because she had no friends
to play with.

? **change**

OLD WORDS:
RULES: **tidy**   <WALTER applies a set of rules
                                   tidy up the text by, for
                                   example, deleting one of a
                                   pair of consecutive identical
                                   words ('a a' in this example).
                                   The child accepts or rejects
                                   each change.>

Once there was a pretty princess. The princess
lived in a big castle in a forest. The forest was
dark. She was lonely because she had no friends
to play with.

? **change**

OLD WORDS:

RULES: **combine**   <A prewritten rule for sentence
                                   combining. The child accepts or
                                   rejects each offered
                                   transformation.>

Once there was a pretty princess who lived in a
big castle in a dark forest. She was lonely because
she had no friends to play with.

'Combine' applies three transformation rules: a 'reduced relative' rule to produce
'Once there was a pretty princess. The princess lived in a big castle in a dark
forest.'; a 'relative' rule to produce: 'Once there was a pretty princess which
lived in a big castle in a dark forest', and a 'who' rule (which alters the 'which'

following a 'human' noun), to produce the final transformed sentence. Normally, the child would try out prewritten rules rather than create her own, but in the example below the child investigates the effect of swapping pairs of nouns in a sentence by calling the command 'rule' to create a new transformation rule:

Once there was a pretty princess who lived in a big castle in a dark forest. She was lonely because she had no friends to play with.

? **rule**

RULE NAME: **swap**

OLD WORDS: **noun1 ??1 noun2** <The double question mark
NEW WORDS: **noun2 ??1 noun1**   matches any sequence of words
within a sentence and that
sequence is used in the
transformed sentence>

Once there was a pretty castle who lived in a big princess in a dark forest. She was lonely because she had no friends to play with.

The rule only operates within a sentence. Thus 'castle' and 'princess' are swapped, but not 'forest' and 'friends'. Further commands transfer text to and from files. There is also an on-line thesaurus that can be called from within WALTER:

? **thesaurus**

WORD TO BE LOOKED UP: **big**

---

big: large, huge, gigantic, giant, important

5.4 NETTY

The NETTY program is similar in design to the many 'Adventure Games', in which a player commands the program to explore an environment in search of treasure. The environment has the structure of an associative network, with nodes representing locations, linked by arcs representing either passages or directions of travel. Each location has a written description and may contain objects. Fig. 5.1 shows a small set of linked locations that correspond to the dialogue below:

? **adventure**

You are standing on a beach to the south of a steep hill. A path leads west.

You can see:
   Box of matches

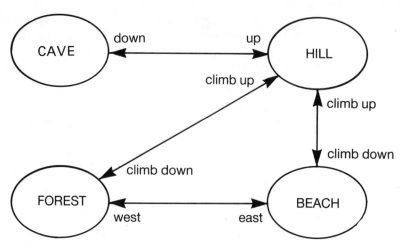

Fig. 5.1 — A network for an adventure game.

What do you want to do? **take the box of matches**
Ok

What do you want to do? **go west**

You are in a forest at the foot of a steep hill. Paths lead off in all directions.

You can see:
    Small twigs

What do you want to do? **take the small twigs**
Ok

What do you want to do? **climb a tree**

The branches are too high to reach.

What do you want to do? **climb the hill**
You are standing on the side of a steep hill above a sandy beach. A small hole leads into the hillside.

What do you want to do? **enter the hole**

You are in a cave set in the hillside. A light shines dimly through a small hole far above you. It is dark in here. If you go on you may fall down a pit.

What do you want to do? **light the twigs**
You are now holding a flaming torch.

NETTY differs from the conventional Adventure game in that a child can easily extend the environment, adding new locations, objects and commands. The user types 'create' and then is guided through the necessary steps:

? **create**

NAME OF LOCATION: **passage**

Type a description of the passage.
DESCRIPTION: **You are crawling through a low North/South passage**
DESCRIPTION:

Now, add after 'OLD WORDS' the commands to move from the passage and after 'NEW WORDS' the location it leads to:

OLD WORDS: ?? **go** ?? **north** ??
NEW WORDS: cave

OLD WORDS: ?? **go** ?? **south** ??
NEW WORDS: lake

OLD WORDS: ?? **stand up** ??
NEW WORDS: **The ceiling here is too low for you to stand.**
OLD WORDS:

Now add the items that can be found in the passage:

ITEM: **Old leather boot**
ITEM:

As in WALTER, double question marks match zero or more words, so '?? go ?? north ??' would match a command like 'go north' or 'please go to the north' and would move the game to the location 'cave'. If the pattern for 'new words' contains more than one word then the text is printed out and the game stays at the same location. The command 'create' is called both to form a new location and to extend an existing one. The 'passage' location needs to be linked to the rest of the game by extending the list of commands for 'cave' to include:

OLD WORDS: ?? **go** ?? **south** ??
NEW WORDS: **passage**

5.5 PHRASEBOOKS AND BOXES

At the next level of detail in the toolkit are the data structures and procedures that drive the programs. To make full use of these a user would need to know the conventions for representing words and simple single-level lists in Logo, but need not understand the programming techniques of iteration or recursion. PAT, WALTER and NETTY store and manipulate data in just two forms: a box and a phrasebook. A box is a simple grouping of items in arbitrary order under a generic name; a box named 'animal' might contain 'cat', 'dog', and 'orang-utang'. This description is completely general, and leaves open the definition of what a box represents, or how it may be used within a toolkit. Thus boxes can stand for taxonomies (Fig. 5.2), concept hierarchies (Fig. 5.3), structured grammars (Fig. 5.4), or any other knowledge structure that holds objects in named classes. They are visual counterparts of mental conceptual classes and, as such, have distinct advantages over other data structures such as strings, records and lists as means of representing linguistic and conceptual knowledge.

A phrasebook is a lookup table of items (or item patterns) and their associates (Fig. 5.5) — words and synonyms; phrases and their foreign equivalents; syntactic patterns and their transformations — and corresponds to conceptual associations.

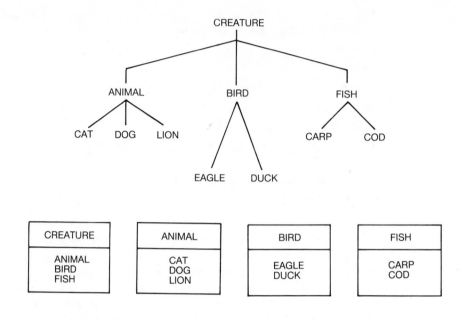

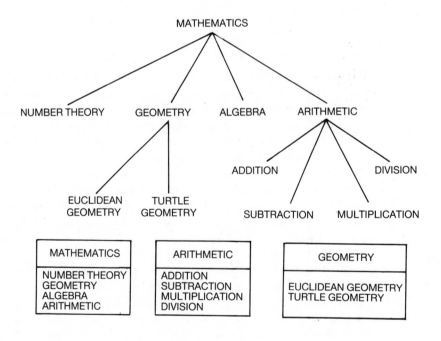

Fig. 5.2 — Representation of a taxonomy as boxes.

Fig. 5.3 — Representation of a concept hierarchy as boxes.

NOUNPHRASE → ARTICLE NOUN/ARTICLE ADJECTIVE NOUN
ARTICLE → A/THE
NOUN → CAT/DOG
ADJECTIVE → FRIENDLY/HAIRY

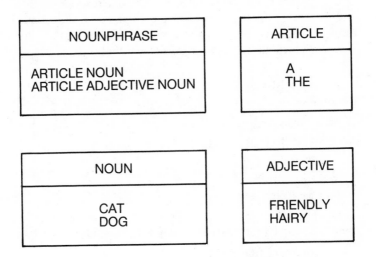

Fig. 5.4 – Representation of a structured grammar as boxes.

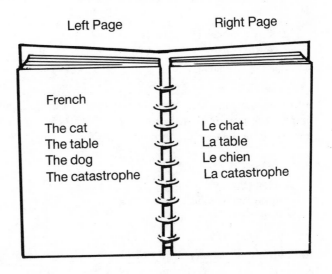

Fig. 5.5 – Entries in a phrasebook.

Both the data structures can be presented in familiar forms. A phrasebook is a direct analogy of a tourist's foreign language phrasebook, with the item to be looked up on the left page and its associate opposite it on the right page. A small set of commands — 'display', 'teach', 'find' and 'forget' — in the form of calls on Logo procedures is sufficient to perform the essential operations. 'display' simply shows the current contents of the phrasebook. 'teach' adds an entry to the book (i.e. the child 'teaches' the computer a phrase and its associate). It accepts either words or lists as arguments and creates an entry in the book (a new entry with the same left page as an existing one overwrites it):

```
?  teach [the dog] [le chien]
?  display
```
the dog   le chien
```
?  teach [the cat] [le chat]
?  display
```
the dog   le chien
the cat   le chat

'find' looks up its argument in the phrasebook and prints the result:

```
?  print find [the dog]
```
le chien
```
?  print find [the horse]
```
the horse is not in the phrasebook

The third command, 'forget', deletes an entry:

```
?  forget [the cat]
?  display
```
the dog   le chien

All these commands can easily be incorporated in Logo procedures to provide a simpler, prompt-driven dialogue ('readlist' is a Logo primitive that reads a line of text typed by the user and forms it into a list):

```
?  to look
>  type [Phrase:]
>  print find readlist
>  end
```

Even in this elementary form, the phrasebook provides an introduction to reference aids and to the techniques of table look-up and pattern-matching. For example, the child might be given a core dictionary or thesaurus that she can extend:

? **look**
Phrase: **sad**
Unhappy, morose, melancholy, depressing, unfortunate
? **look**
Phrase: **wild**
wild is not in the phrasebook

    ? **teach [wild] [untamed, savage, unruly, boisterous]**

With the additional command 'forever' (a primitive in some versions of Logo; easily written in others) a child can produce quizzes or 'conversations':

    ? **teach [what is the capital of france] [paris]**
    ? **teach [hello] [hi there]**
    ? **forever [print find readlist]**

    hello
    hi there
    what is the capital of france
    paris

'Wild cards' for pattern matching are simple, but important, extensions to the phrasebook. A single question mark – ? – matches any single word; a double question mark – ?? – matches a series of words; a question mark followed by one or more letters – ?name, for example – matches a single word and assigns it to a variable (in this case to 'name'); two question marks followed by one or more letters – ??phrase, for example -- matches and assigns a series of words. The child can now create a more general-purpose quiz, or a simple 'Eliza'-type (Weizenbaum, 1976) conversation:

    ? **teach [?? my ?x hurts ??] [your ?x looks very painful]**
    ? **teach [my ?x likes ??y] [tell your ?x to stop ??y and take up jogging instead]**

    ? **forever [print find readlist]**
    doctor, my knee hurts
    your knee looks very painful

    my cat likes programming computers
    tell your cat to stop programming computers and take up jogging instead.

A further extension to the phrasebook turns it into a natural language interface to Logo. If a right page contains Logo commands, then 'find' executes the commands as well as printing them:

    ? **teach [?? area ?? square ? side ?x ?units ??] [type ?x * ?x print ?units]**
    ? **teach [?? area ?? circle ? radius ?r ?units ??] [type 3.141 * ?r * ?r print ?units]**

?   forever [find readline]

what is the area of a square of side 35 cm?
1225 cm

tell me the area of a circle of radius 10 metres
314.1 metres

The box is simply equivalent to a physical box labelled with a single word name and holding an assortment of paper slips. The commands 'display' and 'forget' act as for phrasebooks. 'insert' adds a word, or list of words, to a box:

?   **insert [cat] [noun]**

?   **display**

NOUN

cat

?   **insert [dog][noun]**
?   **display**

NOUN

cat
dog

?   **insert [the noun] [nounphrase]**

?   **display**

NOUN
cat
dog

NOUNPHRASE
the noun

'Scan' scans the 'word pattern' given as input, replacing each box name with one of its contents, chosen at random. The scanning is repeated until no box name remains:

?   **print scan [nounphrase chases nounphrase]**
the cat chases the dog

As with the phrasebook we can write a controlling 'forever' command:

?   **insert [hen] [noun]**
?   **insert [nounphrase chases nounphrase] [sentence]**
?   **forever [print scan readlist]**
sentence

the hen chases the dog

sentence around the farm

the cat chases the hen around the farm

5.6 THE STRUCTURE OF THE PROGRAMS

The PAT program consists of little more than 'insert' and 'scan'. wrapped in another layer of Logo code that issues prompts and calls the procedures. The version of PAT that accepts semantic markers is a little more complex. It calls a modified 'insert' procedure which takes three inputs: a box name, its contents, and a list of meaning tags.

```
?   insert [simile] [parta #1 is like partb #1] [  ]
?   insert [parta] [my noun] [abstract]
?   insert [parta] [your noun] [abstract]
?   insert [partb] [a noun] [inanimate]
?   insert [noun] [joy] [abstract happy]
?   insert [noun] [happiness] [abstract happy]
?   insert [noun] [sorrow] [abstract sad]
?   insert [noun] [anguish] [abstract sad]
?   insert [noun] [sadness] [abstract sad]
?   insert [noun] [lonliness] [abstract sad]
?   insert [noun] [voice] [abstract hear]
?   insert [noun] [gift] [inanimate happy]
?   insert [noun] [blossom] [inanimate happy]
?   insert [noun] [symphony] [inanimate happy hear]
?   insert [noun] [trumpet] [inanimate hear]
?   insert [noun] [wasteland] [inanimate sad]
?   insert [noun] [tombstone] [inanimate sad]
```

'create' scans along its word pattern and, when a box name is found, calls a sub-procedure which recursively generates a list of terminal words and returns these, plus any meaning tags associated with boxes at lower levels of the recursive call. If the box name is followed by a match number (e.g. #1) then the lower level meanings, plus any passed down from higher levels are associated with the number. When the scan then reaches a box name with the corresponding match number then the box item chosen is that which has the greatest intersection between its meanings and those previously associated with the number. If the entire pattern is given a meaning tag then its meanings are added to those of the match number when choosing an item. An example may make the algorithm clearer. Given the procedure call:

```
?   print scan [simile] [  ]
```

the program chooses one from the simile box at random. In this case there is only one item, the pattern [parta #1 is like partb #1]. The pattern is scanned and the first box name encountered is 'parta', with the match number #1. 'parta' contains two items and, since there are no meaning constraints active, then one is chosen at random, say 'your noun'. Its meaning [abstract] is stored.

'Your noun' is scanned and an item is generated from the 'noun' box. Since the meaning 'abstract' is present then only a noun with the tag 'abstract' is picked, say 'sorrow'. Its meanings [abstract sad] are merged with [abstract] to form [abstract sad] and these are passed back to the top level and associated with #1. The scanning of [parta #1 is like partb #1] continues until the next box name 'partb' is found. This also has a #1 marker so the meanings associated with #1, [abstract sad], are passed down. 'partb' contains only one item, the pattern [a noun], so this is chosen. It has the meaning 'inanimate' which is added to the front of the meaning list, producing [inanimate abstract sad]. The pattern 'a noun' is now scanned and the name 'noun' found. An item must be chosen from the noun box that agrees in meaning with [inanimate abstract sad]. Preference is always given to any item that matches the first element of the list, 'inanimate' in this case, since that is the one most recently inherited. Of those nouns with the meaning 'inanimate', only 'wasteland' and 'tombstone' match either 'abstract' or 'sad', so one of the two is picked, producing the final sentence: 'Your sorrow is like a wasteland'. If 'scan' is given a meaning list, then the entire sentence is constrained to match it:

? **print scan [simile. simile.] [happy]**
My joy is like a gift. My happiness is like a symphony.

? **print scan [simile] [hear]**
Your voice is like a trumpet.

WALTER employs the phrasebook as its data structure. A WALTER rule is just a phrasebook entry, with the added power that it may match a part of speech, and the 'rule' command calls the 'teach' procedure to add a new phrasebook entry. Instead of matching the entries on the left page of the phrasebook against the request, the 'change' command moves the left side ('old words') of a rule through the text attempting to find a string of words that matches the rule pattern. Immediately a match is found, the text is transformed into that held on the right side ('new words') of the rule. Associated with each word in the text is part of speech, which was found by a procedure that automatically looks up the word in a phrasebook containing entries such as:

boy   noun human
cry   verb ¦ noun   <'cry' can be either a verb or a noun>

If the word in the text contains affixes then these are stripped off before searching for the part of speech, so the word 'cries' would be converted to 'cry' before being matched against the phrasebook. The part of speech is then converted by another procedure to the correct form of the affix (in this case 'verb third¦noun plural) and associated with the word. Given the rule:

noun1 ??1 noun2   noun2 ??1 noun1

and the text:

The boy sees a girl sitting on a bench. The boy sits down beside the girl.

the left side of the rule is moved along the text until a match is found:

noun1　　　　|————??1—————|　　noun2
boy (noun human) sees (verb third) a (article) girl (noun human)

This is changed to:

noun 1　　　　|————??1——————|　　noun1
girl (noun human) sees (verb third) a (article) boy (noun human)

The matching continues. 'bench' and 'boy' are not swapped since a rule only operates within a sentence (unless the left side of the rule contains an explicit sentence boundary indicated by a full stop) but 'boy' and 'girl' in the second sentence are interchanged, producing the transformed sentence:

The girl sees a boy sitting on a bench. The girl sits down beside the boy.

Rules may be grouped together, in which case each is applied in turn. 'Combine', for sentence combining, consists of five rules:

(1)　??1 noun1 ??2 . article1 noun1 ??3 [verb1 link] adjective1 .
　　　→　　　　??1 adjective1 noun1 ??3 ??2 .

(2)　??1 noun1 ??2 . article1 noun1 ??3 [verb1 link]
　　　preposition1 ??4
　　　→　　　　??1 noun1 ??3 preposition1 ??4 ??2 .

(3)　??1 noun1 ??2 . article1 noun1 ??3 [verb1 link]
　　　participle1 ??4.
　　　→　　　　??1 noun1 ??3 participle1 ??4 ??2 .

(4)　??1 noun1 ??2 . article1 noun1 ??3 .
　　　→　　　　??1 noun1 which ??3 ??2 .

(5)　[noun1 human] which
　　　→　　　　noun1 who

The first three apply a 'reduced relative rule' to sentences containing link verbs (such as 'was'). Thus rule 2 would operate on the sentences 'The cat likes the milk. The cat is on the mat.' to change them to 'The cat on the mat likes the milk.' Rule 4 combines sentences to form 'which' relative clauses and rule 5 ensures that 'which' after a human noun is altered to 'who'. These rules are not infallible but they, and the others used during the project, coped successfully on a wide range of children's texts, and will operate on complex sequences of sentences.

> The building towered above the tenements. The building was gleaming. The building was new. The building was rising high into the sky. The tenements were in the slums. The tenements were decrepit.

As an illustration, the 'combine' rule transforms the sentence above, from a textbook on sentence combining, into:

> The gleaming new building rising high into the sky towered above the tenements. The decrepit tenements were in the slums.

The thesaurus that can be invoked from WALTER is yet another phrasebook, containing entries such as:

> big   large, huge, gigantic, giant, important

The NETTY adventure game is built out of phrasebooks and boxes. Each location (a node in the network) comprises a piece of text, a box containing the items to be found there, and a phrasebook specifying the links to adjacent nodes. For example, a location 'beach' might consist of the text 'You are standing on a sandy beach below a steep cliff. To the west is a forest.', a box containing 'rope' and 'driftwood' and a phrasebook with the entry:

> ?? go ?? west   forest
> ?? climb ?? cliff   clifftop
> swim   The water is too cold to swim.

Whenever the player issues a command, such as 'go to the west', this is looked up in the phrasebook and if a match is found then the next location (here 'forest') is retrieved and the game moves on. If the right page contains more than one word then its message is printed and the location remains the same. A more experienced user can create conditional responses by including Logo code on the right page:

> ?? climb ?? cliff   if holding? [[rope]] then [[clifftop]] else
>   [[beach print [The cliff is too steep to climb]]]

In addition, the program keeps a phrasebook and box for the player, the box holding any items that the player has picked up and the phrasebook containing on the left general commands that apply to any location, and on the right a call to a corresponding Logo procedure:

take the ??x   pickup [??x]
give up   print [game finished] toplevel

The phrasebook and the box are general-purpose data structures with applications beyond text processing (Chapter 7 mentions some further projects). At the next level down is the programming language itself, in this case Logo. A many-layered program allows people to work at their own level of competence: a beginner can operate the ready-made programs WALTER, PAT and NETTY to create, transform and explore language; a more skilled user can call on the phrasebooks and boxes as building blocks to extend the range of activities; an experienced programmer can edit the Logo procedures, alter the prompts and presentation, and design new tools.

6

Teaching Scheme

The two themes developed so far — an understanding of children's development of writing abilities, and computer models of thought and language — have been combined in a teaching scheme for language exploration and creative writing, loosely based on *Language in Use*. The test of an educational innovation, however well-grounded, is in its use with learners in a realistic setting. Since it was not possible to take sufficiently powerful computers into the school classroom, the children came to the computers. The Artificial Intelligence Department at Edinburgh University has a room set apart for educational projects and six children visited it each week to take part in the project.

The teaching scheme is presented in two parts. In the first part, the child starts to acquire an explicit rule knowledge of language, building up an active vocabulary of linguistic terms and finding concrete representations of abstract concepts. The child also explores the basic processes of writing, through a series of games and exercises for generating and transforming text. In each of these she creates, compares, and choses language, so as, for example, to produce a silly story or to complete a 'sentence crossword'.

In the second part of the scheme, a child applies this knowledge of language to creative writing. She follows a path up through the levels of text from sentence to story by creating simple descriptions, linking them together into a descriptive environment, and then forming this into a narrative essay. Along the way guided writing activities encourage her to:

(1) discover and employ new words, sentence structures, scripts and schemas.
(2) generate and transform language at all text levels.

(3) gain a clearer understanding of the audience and function of her writing and use this understanding to select appropriate forms of language.

The project was limited to teaching narrative and descriptive writing, for a single audience, the child's classmates. The first part of the scheme, however, provides a general preparation for creative writing and the second part could be extended to cover other written forms.

Worksheets set down core teaching material, games, exercises, and assessment questions. All the information needed to carry out an activity, including operation of the computer, was contained in the sheets, so they provided a self-teaching package that allowed each child to progress at an individual pace.

Each worksheet introduced a new topic. It began with a resumé of the concept or skill and examples of its use. This was followed by a set of activities whereby the child could assimilate the concept or practise the skill. The early activities were carefully defined but, as the child became more adept, so the support was withdrawn, allowing her to discover her own contexts or applications. The worksheets formed the outline of a teaching scheme, but some detail was omitted. The creative writing projects were deliberately not specified, so as to leave them open to the interests of the individual children. Other activities, particularly the non-computer games, were introduced verbally to the children but could be included in a revised set of worksheets.

The project was supported by three programs — PAT, WALTER and FANTASY — the latter being similar to NETTY in that it enables a child to create and run Adventure games, but with a restricted set of commands:

Room	— What room am I in?
Inhabitants	— What inhabitants does this room currently have?
Objects	— What treasure can I see?
Health $<n>$	— What is the health of inhabitant $<n>$?
Possessions $<n>$	— What does inhabitant $<n>$ possess?
Attack $<n>$	— Attack inhabitant $<n>$.
Take $<n>$	— Take object $<n>$
Drop $<n>$	— Drop $<n>$th possession.
Exits	— What are the exits from this room?
Quit	— Leave the game.

Some features of FANTASY not found in NETTY include the ability to give doors and objects 'difficulty levels'; the higher the level, the more attempts are needed to see an object or pass through a door. Additional players can be specified and the computer controls them by moving them at random through the environment. The scheme only required the children to operate the programs at the top, prompt-driven level, so there was no need to teach programming skills, nor to write the programs in a language suitable for children. In fact WALTER and PAT were written in POP-2 and Fantasy was written in C.

Six eleven-year-old children (three boys and three girls) chosen at random from an inner city primary school formed the experimental group and a similar group of children was given normal classroom teaching, plus occasional visits to the Artificial Intelligence Department for computer-based work unrelated to

English. Shortly after the start of the project, one boy from the control group left the school, so reducing its size to five children. Their class teacher offered a brief character sketch of each child in the experimental group:

Sharon: Intelligent but domineering. A ready talker and leader.

Dorothy: Sparodically imaginative and creative. Competes with Sharon for attention. No exposure to books, except through school.

Louise: Quiet, methodical and intelligent.

James: Somewhat shy. From a professional family. Moderately intelligent. Is exposed to books at home.

Kevin: Confident and 'street wise'. A local boy, from an affluent family. No exposure to books at home.

Derek: Erratic temperament and a slow learner.

6.1 DESIGN

The children took part in the investigation over three school terms, from September 1979 to June 1980. The sessions were held in the Department of Artificial Intelligence and each one lasted for 60–70 minutes. While they were absent, the remaining children were given normal classroom work (which included an occasional English lesson) by their teacher. By the end of the first part of the scheme it was clear that two of the six children, Kevin and Derek, had little ability to explore language and even less enthusiasm, so they were given separate writing activities, while the other four children continued with the second part of the course.

The control group had three sessions at the Department, to meet myself and overcome resentment at not being included in the project, which might otherwise have affected their test performance. They followed a teaching scheme prepared for the Logo project (du Boulay and O'Shea, 1976), writing simple computer programs in Logo to draw shapes. Like the experimental group, they used computers as a learning aid, but in a different subject area. The two groups came together for the final essays.

6.2 EVALUATION

An 'illuminative evaluation' 'whose primary concern is with description and interpretation rather than measurement and prediction' (Parlett and Hamilton, 1972) was more appropriate than a psychometric evaluation. We are interested in more than just the aggregate end results of the teaching scheme; we want also to understand the means by which a child becomes a mature writer, the effect of each part of the teaching scheme on the children's understanding and control of language, and the variation in skills and learning strategies amongst the children. We need therefore to monitor the progress of individual children. Case studies can illuminate the *learning process* and so tell more about the relation between teaching and language development than measures of *learning outcome*.

As teacher and resource, I made no attempt to remain distant and uninvolved. I observed the children throughout the investigation and wrote a report on each session. Every piece of writing, including notes, rough drafts and computer printouts, was collected and filed along with the completed worksheets.

All the children were asked to write four essays, two before the start of the investigation, and two at the end. They were produced under classroom test conditions, with a fixed tome of 45 minutes per essay. Each child was asked to produce a narrative and a descriptive essay, on a topic chosen and introduced by the author:

Pre Test   — Descriptive Essay: 'A Visit to the Department'

Pre Test   — Narrative Essay: 'An Adventure While Travelling'

Post Test — Descriptive Essay: 'A Fair'

Post Test — Narrative Essay: 'An Island Adventure'

Three methods of evaluation were used. First, the writing process of the children in the experimental group was assessed throughout the project. Second, the pre and post essays from both groups were rated independently by two teachers of English for overall quality. Third, both sets of essays were subjected to a feature analysis.

To profit from the teaching scheme, a child should already have a tacit rule knowledge of language. Without this, a child would be unable to follow the activities which involve language manipulation and the recognition of syntactic patterns. Children should be reaching this stage of language development around the age of eleven, so we would expect a sharp division in the experimental group, between those children who cannot cope with the linguistic demands of the scheme and those who enjoy and benefit from the opportunity to experiment with language.

We would not expect the experimental group children to write as well in the pre and post essays as they did during the project, when there was ample time for planning and revision. Nevertheless, there should be some transfer of skills from the teaching scheme, so the post essays of those children who completed the scheme should contain 'mature' features not found in their earlier essays.

As for the teachers' ratings of the essays, we would not expect the duration of the scheme and the size of the groups to be sufficient for any statistically significant difference to be found between the mean scores of the control and experimental groups.

The different methods of assessment should be regarded as spotlights, illuminating aspects of children's writing abilities. Taken together, they should indicate: first, the child's process of writing; second, the particular styles and techniques of writing that a child employs; third, the overall quality of each child's written productions. This profile is useful both for assessing the writing development of a group of children, and for diagnosing a particular child's preoccupations and weaknesses.

6.3 DESCRIPTION OF THE SESSIONS

The first worksheet contrasted the word structure of a sentence with a random word sequence; it demonstrated that language consists of more than a random string of words, and accustomed the child to using a computer. The children were read a story about a woman named Pat who had constructed a machine to generate random strings of words. A question in the worksheet then asked 'Do you think that Pat's machine would write good poetry? Why?'.

The children's answers to this first question indicates their differences in aptitude. Dorothy, Louise, James, and Sharon all answered 'No', replying 'The machine is stupid'; 'All it would do was drop the words out one by one'; 'The words might be in a muddle'; 'It only brought out the words she had made. It wasn't doing anything'. Kevin and Derek, however, both decided that Pat's imaginary machine could write good poetry 'because it can do all sorts of complicated things' and 'because it is a good idea how to use a machine to write poetry'.

The children then worked in pairs to produce similar 'poems' to Pat's, by placing cards, each containing a single word, in a 'word box' and then taking them out again in random order. None had any difficulty with this exercise and all produced random sequences of 15 words for the worksheet. They then carried out a similar exercise using the PAT program on the computer. They typed words into the program's 'word box' and generated 'poems' containing those words, specifying the number of lines in the poem and the number of words per line. Three terminals were available to the project, so the children normally worked in pairs, taking turns at typing.

Although none of the children had previously used a computer, nor had they learned to type, they found few difficulties in operating the program. The only recurrent problem was caused by a child forgetting to press the 'return' button at the end of each line of input. By the middle of the second session the children had generated some simple 'poems' and had begun to create more varied vocabularies by swapping terminals and adding to each other's lists.

After playing a board game called Context, a sentence version of Scrabble where words must be added to those on the table to form sentences, the children began the second worksheet. They sorted the 'word box' into separate 'part of speech boxes', creating one box for each part of speech, and then formed the parts of speech into patterns which would generate sentences and poems. The first few they generated by pulling out the words from the appropriate boxes and then, once they understood the process, they typed in the boxes and patterns to the PAT program.

The last exercise in Worksheet 2, a sentence crossword (Fig. 6.1), is a useful diagnostic test of language manipulation. Each child worked on this exercise alone, (except in the case of Kevin, who was helped to choose parts of speech) yet each carried out a sequence of operations in the same order:

(1) Choose the correct part of speech.
(2) Make transitive/intransitive verb substitutions.

(3) Alter words to improve meaning.

(4) Alter words so that verbs agree with nouns in number.

ARTICLE	ADJECTIVE	NOUN	VERB	PARTICLE	ADJECTIVE	NOUN
NOUN	////	VERB	////	ADJECTIVE	NOUN	VERB
VERB	////	ARTICLE	////	NOUN	VERB	ADVERB
////	ARTICLE	NOUN	ADVERB	VERB	////	////

5. CAN YOU COMPLETE THIS CROSSWORD BY FILLING IN A WORD FOR EACH PART OF SPEECH, SO THAT THE SENTENCES ACROSS AND DOWN ALL MAKE SENSE?

Fig. 6.1 — Sentence crossword.

The children progressed different amounts along this sequence. Kevin (with some assistance) chose the correct parts of speech, but made no further changes. James at first chose some incorrect parts of speech. He altered some, for example 'meat' to 'bites', but let others remain unchanged. Sharon chose correct parts of speech, then altered the intransitive verb 'glows' to the transitive verb 'hears', changing 'moon glows the sea' to 'moon hears the sea'. Louise also changed a verb and then improved the sense of a connecting sentence, from 'the white moon has a old dog' to 'the white man has a old dog'. In addition to these Dorothy also made a series of changes to ensure agreement in number: 'dog' to 'dogs' and 'moves' to 'move'. Her completed crossword is reproduced as Fig. 6.2.

The children spent the next two sessions as journalists, producing a two-page newspaper. Its content was determined largely by the children, who also took the photographs and laid out the pages. As well as giving them a break from the worksheets, it provided a purpose for writing and a well-defined audience, their classmates. The newspaper was photocopied and circulated around the school. Although some of the children copied out their articles to fit the format of the newspaper, their only revisions were an occasional correction of spelling.

The next worksheet contained a story with parts of speech in place of some words:

This is a tale about a **adjective** man called Mr **name** who lives **adverb** in a **adjective** house with a **noun**, two **nouns** and a **adjective noun**. He often **verb adverb** as he is an extremely **adjective** person. Every morning he **verb** and then **verb adverb** out of the window. On Sundays he **verb** to his next door neighbour Mrs **name** who **verb** back to him.

ARTICLE	ADJECTIVE	NOUN	VERB	ARTICLE	ADJECTIVE	NOUN
the	silent	·people	see	the	white	moon's
NOUN		VERB·		ADJECTIVE	NOUN	VERB
moon		see		black	people	move
VERB		ARTICLE		NOUN	VERB	ADVERB
glows		the		dogs	drink	quickly
	ARTICLE	NOUN	ADVERB	VERB		
	the	moon's	quickly	move		

Fig. 6.2 – Dorothy's completed sentence crossword.

The children recalled the story from a PAT library file and then instructed the program to complete the story by substituting words for the appropriate parts of speech, e.g.: 'This is a tale about a sad man called Mr Periwinkle who lives stupidly in a tall house . . .'. They then made up a story outline of their own, to be filled in by the program. Sharon and Louise enjoyed experimenting with this program and together made up the following outline: 'One day a 'adjective' 'noun' was walking in the 'noun' when she found a door. She went 'preposition' and saw a 'adjective' lady.'

It was clear from the first session onwards that Derek and Kevin were gaining little from the scheme. They appeared to regard the games and exercises as pointless and had little enthusiasm for operating the computer, often disrupting these sessions with loud conversation and horseplay. By contrast, the other children were enthusiastic, to varying degrees, about investigating language by computer. Dorothy in particular showed a marked improvement in interest and attention during the first part of the scheme.

During session 10, the children were given a diagnostic test of language manipulation skills (Appendix 2). The test confirmed the impression that Derek and Kevin were having problems in following the teaching scheme, and they were not taken on to the second part. Instead, they usually visited the Department at different times from the rest of the group and used the computer as a simple word processor, typing in text, altering spelling and then printing out a neat copy. They were still not enjoying the work and, rightly, suspected that the exercises were designed mainly to keep them quiet and occupied. On the penultimate session, however, they were asked to write a short contribution to the children's page of the local newspaper, on the theme 'Who I would most like to be'. Both children refused to consider the possibility that their work might be published in a 'real newspaper', until I pointed out that they would have the advantage over other children of sending neat, tidied, typewritten copy. For the first time, some spark of interest gleamed and both boys applied themselves to the task, producing these passages:

> I would like to be Archie McPherson [a Scottish football commentator] because I would like to see all of the football matches. And I would be able to meet all the Football players and talk to them. And I would be able to get all the autographs and give them to my children. (Derek).

> I would like to be JR because of all the fame and fortune. Look at all the TV programmes he has been on and he has made a lot of money out of that series. That is why I would like to be JR. (Kevin).

To their delight, both offerings were printed in the newspaper and, encouraged by their class teacher, Derek later wrote letters to other organisations.

6.4 CREATIVE WRITING

The four remaining members of the experimental group began work on the second part of the scheme, which applied their knowledge of language to creative writing. The worksheets covered two functional forms of writing – descriptive and narrative – and concentrated on particular stylistic or structural aspects, such as word choice, repetition, and imprecision. These were integrated with writing projects which led the child from simple descriptions to a narrative essay.

The first worksheet of the section gave an introduction to the process of 'generate and select', described in Chapter 2. The worksheets began at the word, rather than plan, level in order to introduce the process through readily understood examples. Exercises to choose amongst story plans (for example a 'Story Maker' game described in Chapter 4) would demand of the child a more abstract level of evaluation. Instead, planning is introduced at a later point in the scheme, when its purpose and operation are clearer to the children.

The worksheet presented a short passage with a choice of words available at approximately every tenth word. An extract is given below:

```
            beach                          deep blue
On the shore of the tropical island, where  soaking wet waters
            sand                          strong silent

                          sailor                   watching
   lapped the white shore, a lone   man   stood. He was  looking
                          seafarer                  seeing

   at a rowing boat draw farther and farther away from him, heading
```

tall ship   bay.
for the huge sailing ship which stood at anchor in the ocean.
big boat   water.

At each of these points the child selects the word or phrase which best suits the story. The children worked in pairs and then compared results, in a lively discussion with plausible reasons offered for the word choices:

> I chose 'water' not 'ocean' because 'ocean' means it's too far out to sea to anchor. (Dorothy).

> 'Seafarer' is better than 'sailor' because it's old-fashioned and the picture is of an old-fashioned boat. (Louise).

For the next activity, pairs of children carried out a similar process on the computer. A set of rules for the PAT program generated alternative versions of a ghost story. The children could select a sentence from the story and display as many versions as they wished (since a sentence may have up to 12 decision points, each with a choice of three words, the number of possible versions was large). Although the children were exhorted to be critical of the computer's choice of words, and to produce better alternatives, they generally wrote down one of those offered by the program. The exception was Dorothy who made up her own words (in italics below) to fit slots in the following sentences:

> I was thinking about *riding* to my mate's house which was nearby.
> Then we would continue on to the stream and *feed the horses*.

The exercise was, in general, successful, though the children were required to make too many decisions and so sometimes became restless and lost the flow of narrative.

The next worksheet covered simple description. It began with a game which asked children to create interesting descriptive sentences, avoiding their normal uninspired clutch of modifiers: 'big', 'nasty', 'horrible', etc. A PAT library file contained a series of boxes which substituted an asterisk for an adjective and an exclamation mark for an adverb, for example:

BOX NAME	CONTENTS
big	*
quickly	!
nasty	*

As the program only recognised some 200 words, the purpose of the game was to 'outwit' the machine by inventing sentences with unusual modifiers which would not be substituted by the program. The worksheet gave core sentences to be embellished, for example:

> The aeroplane flew under the bridge.

If the child changes this to:

> The tiny aeroplane flew swiftly under the low bridge

the program would substitute for 'tiny' and 'low' but not 'swiftly' producing

The * aeroplane flew swiftly under the * bridge.

The children all worked enthusiastically to produce such ornate sentences as:

The acrobatic jet fighter went shooting under the huge, old fashioned railway bridge. (James).

The young curious girl looked inquiringly at the old victorian house. (Dorothy).

The elderly crazy looking man sat on the green bench snoozing. (Sharon).

The old grey-haired man sat uncomfortably on the old uneven wooden bench. (Louise).

The game element of the program contributed to its attraction, particularly the opportunity it gave to 'beat the computer'.

From there the writing activities led to simple descriptions, of exhibits in the Edinburgh Waxworks Museum. The children were told beforehand that the group would tour the museum and that each child should pick a single waxwork and make notes on it, from which a full description would be written the following week. The descriptions could be included in the class newspaper. The children were informally introduced to story planning, by being asked to take notes as an aid to memory.

The children all opted for waxworks in the Chamber of Horrors and assiduously wrote details of their dress, features and surroundings. All four children referred to the museum guide book for background information and during the next session they were encouraged to study their notes and reorder them to improve the flow and logic of the description. At this point they were introduced to a thesaurus, in book form, with the suggestion that they avoid the repetition of common words by finding synonyms.

Dorothy made considerable changes to her initial draft. She compressed jumbled and repetitive notes on her observations of the waxwork and padded out a two sentence entry in the museum guide book with her own imaginings. The first draft and the version printed in the newspaper (version 3) are given below:

Hook Victim

Yuch,

The hook is through his stomach. his tongue is hanging out there is blood coming down from his mouth.

This was an Algerian divice. The victim was impaled upon a hook and left hanging in the open until he died.

This man's body was in pain the hook was right inside and back out again.

This mans face was a horrible looking face his tongue was hanging out and his eyes were blood-shot, and were half hanging out of his head. he is lying with the hook in the front of his stomach and he is not balanced on. (First draft).

The Hook Victim

This man must be in pain there is a hook through his stomach. His tongue is hanging out. His eyes have turned white and have red lines through them. He would not give evidence against the person he was working for. So he was given as much time as he wanted to make his mind up. But the police got fed up waiting so they took the victim into the open and left him hanging until he was dead. He was left hanging with a hook through him. He had nothing to balance on except his legs, but even they were rotting away. (Final version).

At sentence level, she apparently found difficulty in combining the present tense of her observations with the past tense of the guide book, but solved the problem by changing the tense of the end description to fit the preceding sentences: 'He has nothing to balance him except his legs and they were rotting through' (version 2); 'He had nothing to balance on except his legs, but even they were rotting away' (version 3). In Chapter 2 we suggested that deletion of text in successive redrafts may be one indication of a mature writer and of the four children, only Dorothy rejected substantial sections of text in redrafting.

Of the other three children, Sharon called on the thesaurus to simplify text from the museum handbook and to embellish her own notes and James reordered his notes, adding a section from the handbook. For her article on the waxwork, Louise extracted the salient facts from a 450-word passage in the museum handbook and restated its more flamboyant sections in her own concise style. For example, she compressed 48 words into 25, with little loss of detail:

> Briefly, it was their custom to lie in wait by the public highway to attack and kill passers-by, and then consume their bodies and use their belongings as best they could. What they could not eat at once they pickled in brine and preserved for future use. (Handbook).

> They were cannibals and they ate anyone who came by. If they were full they put what they had left in a jar and pickled it. (Louise).

All six children spent the next four sessions in producing another issue of the newspaper. It contained the descriptions of the waxworks, plus interviews with staff members of the Department (the staff were most tolerant towards children who accosted them for details of research projects, and they provided some quite revealing information).

Session 21 brought in the importance of audience to descriptive writing. James was absent, so Sharon and Dorothy worked together and Louise worked alone. Each team was shown two different photographs (one black and white, and one colour) and asked to write descriptions of them. The descriptions were passed to the other team who attempted to redraw the picture. If a team had problems in following the description then it was passed back to be redrafted. This exercise provoked a useful discussion about a reader's knowledge and about descriptive completeness. The description by Sharon and Dorothy of their colour picture (a illustration of a Martian monster from a science fiction comic) omitted any mention of colour, and Louise complained that she could not draw the picture as she had no idea of which coloured crayons to use. Both groups caused protest by leaving out the size and orientation of parts of their pictures. The discussion led to a list of ingredients for detailed descriptions, such as colour, size, and shape.

Up until this stage in the seheme, the children had produced every piece of writing in longhand, using the computer only for games and exercises. They were now taught to use the WALTER program as an aid to drafting and revision. The children found no problems in using the program and welcomed the opportunity to revise text without defacing the page or rewriting an entire passage. Sharon remarked 'It's good. You can make as many changes as you want and you always get a neat one at the end'.

A thesaurus program can be called from within WALTER, and the children developed a 'synonym game'. The players worked in pairs. One person thought of a common word which was typed to the computer. In the ten seconds, or thereabouts, that the program took to reply with a list of synonyms, the other player wrote down as many related words as possible. One point was scored for each related word and two points for one which was not in the program's thesaurus. The children used their own judgement about whether a word was related or not. This game proved popular, due again to the opportunity of beating the computer.

The final worksheet, entitled 'Lazy Words', covered imprecision in writing. The children called up a series of transformation rules in the WALTER program, the 'thing' rules, which showed the consequences of imprecision in writing. These rules altered all the nouns in a piece of text to 'lazy words'. The sequence below shows it in operation:

new

STORY: **Once there was a pretty princess who lived in a**
STORY: **big castle in a dark forest. She was very lonely**
STORY: **because she had no friends to play with.**
STORY:

NEW FINISHED

change

OLD WORDS:

RULES: **thing**

Once there was someone pretty who lived in something big in something else which is dark. She was very lonely because she had no people to play with.

Working in pairs, one child recalled one of her own pieces of descriptive writing that had been saved on file and applied the 'thing rules' to it. The other child then looked at the resulting text and tried to reconstruct the original piece.

Transformations like 'Mr Sharples room is quite small, it is square with a sort of cubby-hole which is about the size of a cupboard' into 'Mr Sharples thing is quite small, it is square with a sort of thing which is about something of a thing.' caused much hilarity, while illustrating the need for precision.

For the final part of the scheme, the children progressed from simple descriptions to a descriptive environment and then to a narrative, with the aid of the FANTASY program. The FANTASY network of ordered descriptions acts as a story plan and external memory, and stories arise naturally, as the children play the game and explore the network. By separating a story into two components — a descriptive environment and a route through the environment — the children could create, alter and refer to each in turn, with the computer providing a bridge between description and narrative.

For this project, the children were deliberately given little assistance in forming their individual descriptions, the emphasis being on the relation between them and the structure of the environment. In order to understand the task the children (except for Sharon, who was absent) first played 'Colossal Adventure', a game similar in structure to FANTASY. After some 25 minutes of playing the game the children were prised away from the terminals. I explained that they could create their own Adventure game, from descriptions of rooms, characters and treasure, and suggested 'a haunted house' as the setting. Figs. 6.3 and 6.4 show the development of one game devised jointly by Dorothy and Louise. They first drew a plan of a house, with nine main rooms and many connecting doors, hallways and secret passages (Fig. 6.3). After insisting that they wanted to write the descriptions themselves, they arrived at the next session with details of each room, its contents, and its inhabitants, covering eight sides of A4 paper. One sheet is reproduced as Fig. 6.4.

In both vocabulary and phrasing the girls' Fantasy environment is richer than any of their previous writings, containing the words 'clammy' and 'emporium', and the phrases 'filled with a cold, misty fog', 'a wardrobe to match', 'ripped victorian pictures' and 'happy atmospheric room', all of which indicate a use of language for dramatic effect. The other pair of children devised a less elaborate, but adequate, game of nine rooms.

The children typed in most of their text to WALTER and I then converted the descriptions into input files for FANTASY (unlike NETTY, FANTASY offers no simple set of commands for creating a game). This involved appending list of integers to indicate links between the rooms (taken from the children's original plans) and various properties for the characters and objects, such as size and activity.

When the children returned for the next session, they played the games, their own and other group's and, since values are associated with each piece of treasure, the session became a contest to collect the most valuable hoard of treasure. Below is an extract from the game of Louise and Dorothy:

> You are in a dull, clammy kitchen with a big black stove on a wall. There is a flaming fire on another wall. There is a pane of glass smashed which was in a big window which is all steamed up. There is a sink which is full of dirty dishes.

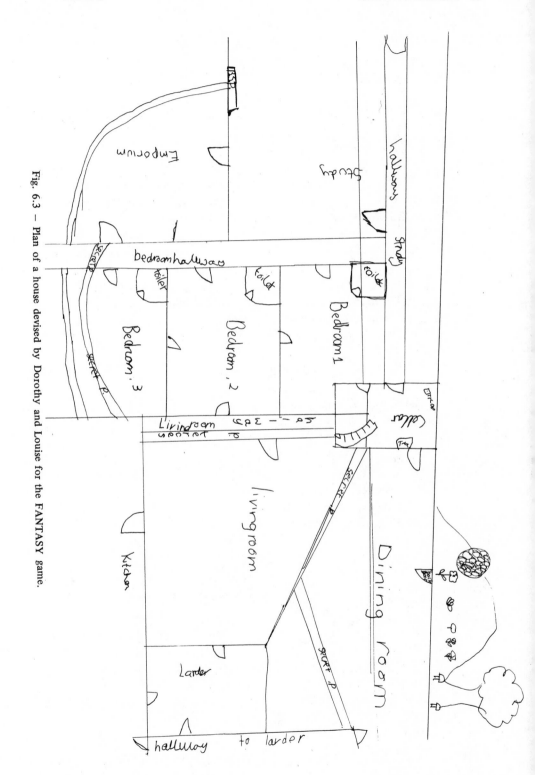

Fig. 6.3 – Plan of a house devised by Dorothy and Louise for the FANTASY game.

Kitchen. ✓

(a) description

A dull, clammy, kitchen with a big black stove
a big flaming fire in one corner, a pane of glass
in a big window which is all steamed up a sink
full of dirty dishes.
a kitchen table has a bottle
of wine un opened the year of the wine is 1883.
Keys to larder are on table. you have found gold.

(b) Things to pick up
a dirty dish
bottle of wine.

Keys to larder
Gold

(c) Exits and Entrances.S.P.

S.P. from study.
S.P. from Emporium.
S.P. to cellar.
door to livingroom
locked door to Larder
door to hallway

(d) People
dazed kitchen maid
strangled cook
∧foot

(e) Events
kitchen maid wakes, suddenly
she is running after you with
a butcher's knife.

continued on page four
otherwise P.T.O.

Fig. 6.4

a secret passage leads west
a wooden door leads northwest
a wooden door leads north
a wooden door leads northeast

The following are also here:
1 – a dazed kitchen maid

a dazed kitchen made has just left through a wooden
door (northeast)

objects
You can see
1 – a dirty dish

north
You are in a bright coloured happy atmospheric room in it there is, two big
lounging chairs bright fabric but damaged, a sofa to match chairs, a coal fire
still burning, a glass coffee table smashed to pieces. keys to the cellar lie
beside it. Ripped victorian pictures are hanging on the walls.

a wooden door leads west
a wooden door leads northeast
a wooden door leads south
a wooden door leads east

The following are also here:
1 – a chef

objects
you can see
1 – a page of diary dated April 10th.
2 – a note saying "Have a glass of wine".

take 1
ok

The game provoked a discussion of story planning. Each run produces a
new narrative and shows that not only can many stories be built around one
environment, but also that the layout of the house and the order in which its
locations are explored can determine the player's interest and suspense: secret
passages may herald treasure, or danger; the object of the search should be well
hidden, far from the entrance and accessible only by a tortuous route; decoy
signs and small pieces of treasure can heighten suspense.

For the final two sessions, the children wrote narrative stories based on their experiences of playing FANTASY. The stories were first handwritten and then typed to the WALTER program. The drafts were returned with my written comments and indications of the sections in need of revision or expansion but no suggestions as to how the revisions should be carried out. Appendix 3 contains the first draft, with the child's own annotations, plus the final version, of each story. Dorothy and Louise worked together, with Louise as writer and Dorothy providing ideas and criticism, while Sharon and James wrote separate stories.

James' story relies on stock images from horror films — butler; blood-covered nail — but fleshed out with details of character and setting:

a poor old man appeared. He said to them in a stubborn croaky voice . . .

The wall had plain whitish wall-paper, but it was a bit grotty with cobwebs and dust.

The narrative links a series of coherent episodes, each set in a different room and sustained across a number of sentences.

Dorothy and Louise referred to their plan of the house, drew a line on it indicating the explorer's progress through the rooms, and then followed this route in their story. A few passages from the game were included, for instance this description of the entrance and butler:

The detective walked up to the wooden porch of the manor. He knocked at the large oak door, the door opened with an enormous creaking sound. An old butler appeared and asked "Whom seeketh thou this evening?" Suddenly! a giant black bat flew down from the lintel above the oak door.

They spent some time in devising an ending for the story with the result that the text was written in some haste, to complete a draft by the end of the session. When this was pointed out to them, the girls rewrote the final section adding two, more detailed, concluding sentences. They also made substantial sentence level revisions to the start of the story and, with the aid of the computer thesaurus, replaced two occurrences of 'big', five of 'walk' and one of 'goes' with synonyms.

Sharon wrote the first draft of her 'Haunted House' story in haste, spilling ideas and impressions onto paper as the opening section below shows. This 'stream of consciousness' style is very different from her previous writings:

I am a detective I have come to the house of mystery because on December the 25th there were strange noises coming from the house. Its probably just bats or rats bit I dont think so the something funny going on the house looks dull and damp. There is a wooden door it looks as if it has not been used for years whats that noise chairs rattling oh god what is this house its getting nearer a man he has no head. Oh god. He didn't see me good. A bedroom cobwebs everywhere click somebody locked me in there is a women at the far end there is a women she is green her teeth are red shes coming for me. Gun weres my gun here bang bang bang bang shes not dead but shes went away the bullets went right through her.

Given the content of the story, a solitary exploration of a haunted house, the style is appropriate and represents a transition towards 'poetic' use of language. That this is deliberate, and not merely the result of haste, is indicated by the subsequent revisions which were substantial, but did not alter the overall style. She rewrote and expanded the first section, added punctuation, and altered words and phrases, for example, 'strange' to 'weird', 'I've fell' to 'I've fallen' and 'He has no head' to 'He's headless'.

6.5 SUMMARY

The monitoring of the children's activities and attitudes to the teaching scheme has generally confirmed expectations. The children formed two distinct groups. Two of the children would only tackle a worksheet if given constant assistance. In part, they were being deliberately disruptive, making a bid for leadership of the group, and they may well have made more progress if left to themselves. Clearly, though, they gained a little from the scheme. They were certainly not overawed by the computers; both boys were eager to show their skills at computer arcade games. Nor were they illiterate; both wrote extended pieces of more than 150 words. To them, writing was an intuitive act and a knowledge of language, was however attractively presented, was irrelevant.

The remaining four children followed the scheme without undue problem. Their questions were almost entirely on language use or the writing topic, rather than how to operate the computer. Having followed the children through the teaching scheme, and shared their excitement and frustrations, it is difficult to judge their attitude towards the experiment. They certainly found sections of the scheme to be tedious and difficult, especially the second worksheet, but the fact that they were each prepared to produce several complete redrafts of articles for the newspaper, without being goaded, that Dorothy and Louise wrote the Fantasy outlines at home, and that all four children had to be persuaded to leave the Fantasy game and return to school, suggests that they enjoyed the activities.

Two children, Sharon and Dorothy, appear to have carried this enthusiasm over to their personal reading. Their class teacher reported on the children's reading habits at the end of the project:

James: Shows no interest [in reading] except when forced.

Dorothy: Interest increased this year. Reading good teenage girls books.

Sharon: Has become dramatically addicted during the year. Progressed through Enid Blyton to good teenage books.

Louise: Still rather immature. Enid Blyton and books aimed at younger children.

Dorothy's progress was particularly satisfying. From a family with few books, she had little incentive to read and had shown no particular interest in reading or writing before the start of the project. However, she possessed a keen analytic mind and her success in the language activities appeared to awake more general interest in language and literature.

6.6 ASSESSMENT OF THE CHILDREN'S WRITINGS

The children wrote a descriptive and a narrative essay at the start of the investigation and two similar essays after the final teaching session. The control group of five children produced essays on the same subjects. The essays have been assessed by two methods — the impressionistic judgements of two independent English teachers, and an analysis of linguistic features — and the results are presented below.

6.6.1 Teachers' assessment

Each child's pre and post essays were marked by two independent teachers, on a scale of 1 to 7 for 'general impression' and on a scale of 1 to 5 in four analytic categories: 'content'; 'organisation', 'appropriateness and style' and 'grammatical conventions'. Table 6.1 shows the rankings from each assessor, based on the combined marks in pre and post essays. A cross indicates that the child was absent and the ranking is based on performance in one essay. A star indicates a child from the experimental group.

A Wilcoxon test shows that the post test scores from each assessor for all eleven children were significantly higher than their pre test scores ($p<0.05$, two-tailed). When the pre and post scores are compared for each group, the control group children show slightly greater gains (a Mann–Whitney test on the ranked data reveals that the difference is not significant ($p<0.05$, two-tailed)). The two analytic categories most relevant to the experiment are 'organisation' and 'style', so the marks for these categories have been combined for each assessor to produce Table 6.2. Again there is no significant difference between the two groups.

An unexpected finding was that the assessors differed over the performance of individual children in the experimental group, particularly in the 'style and organisation' combined category. As Table 6.2 shows, the pre to post rank shifts vary far more for the experimental group than the control group. The assessors were in accord about the performance of Dorothy — she maintained her high rank position — but they differ markedly in their judgements of the essays by the other three children. In the combined 'style' and 'organisation' categories, no child from the control group moved by more than two rank positions from pre to post essay, yet the rank positions of Louise, Sharon, and James all altered by between four and ten places, in different directions and from different assessors. Whenever the rankings of one assessor show a large pre to post movement for a particular child, then the rankings of the other assessor show no movement, or a small shift in the opposite direction.

Table 6.1 — Rankings for 'general impression' category.

	Assessor A		Assessor B	
	Pre essay	Post essay	Pre essay	Post essay
1	Anne	Dorothy*	Louise*	Robert
2	Sharon*	Anne	Robert	Dorothy*
3	Dorothy*	James*	Nigel+	Sharon*
4	Saras	Nigel+	Dorothy*	Saras+
5	Robert	Saras+	Anne	Nigel+
6	Nigel+	Robert	Sharon*	Anne
7	Louise*	Louise*	James*	Louise*
8	Kevin*	Sharon*	Derek*	James*
9	James*	Derek*	Kevin*	Kevin*
10	Derek*	Richard	Saras	Richard
11	Richard	Kevin*	Richard	Derek*

Table 6.2 — Rankings of combined 'organisation' and 'style'.

	Assessor A		Assessor B	
	Pre essay	Post essay	Pre essay	Post essay
1	Nigel+	Dorothy*	Anne	Dorothy*
2	Dorothy*	Nigel+	Dorothy*	Anne
3	Sharon*	Anne	Sharon*	Robert
4	Anne	James*	Louise*	Sharon*
5	Saras	Saras+	Nigel+	Nigel+
6	Kevin*	Robert	Robert	Saras+
7	Louise*	Louise*	James*	Louise*
8	Robert	Richard	Saras	James*
9	Derek*	Kevin*	Kevin*	Kevin*
10	James*	Derek*	Derek*	Richard
11	Richard	Sharon*	Richard	Derek*

6.6.2 Feature analysis

A feature analysis of the essays gives a more detailed profile and Table 6.3 shows the results of the analysis. In each category the scores for the two essays were summed, except for those children (Nigel and Saras) who missed an essay; their single score for that category was doubled.

The post test essays contained more mature feature categories than the pre test ones, for both groups of children, and fewer immature categories. A comparison of the two groups shows that the mean 'mature' scores rose by 5.67 for the experimental group and by 5.00 for the control group. Thus, as expected, the experimental group showed the greater increase, but a *t*-test showed that the difference was not at significance level. For the immature categories, the situation was reversed. The mean 'immature' score dropped by only 0.33 for the experimental group and by 1.80 for the control group. This indicates what we might call a 'Tarzan syndrome': the children are developing mature writing techniques, but have not cast off their old habits. Indeed, the more a child concentrates on adding new features, such as multiple modifiers, the less attention she may devote to the story plan or content. Any global assessment of 'style' or 'organisation' will balance mature and immature aspects of the essay and so may not give due credit to innovation in children's writing.

Table 6.3 – Feature analysis of pre/post essays.

	EXPERIMENTAL GROUP					
	Pre		Post		Difference	
	Mature	Immature	Mature	Immature	Mature	Immature
James	8	9	15	7	+7	−2
Sharon	6	5	13	4	+7	−1
Dorothy	8	9	14	3	+6	−6
Louise	7	6	13	10	+6	+4
Derek	1	5	6	8	+5	+3
Kevin	4	4	7	4	+3	0
MEAN	5.67	6.33	11.33	6	+5.67	−0.33

	CONTROL GROUP					
	Pre		Post		Difference	
	Mature	Immature	Mature	Immature	Mature	Immature
Robert	8	9	15	7	+7	−2
Saras+	4	8	10	6	+6	−2
Richard	4	8	9	7	+5	−1
Nigel+	4	6	8	2	+4	−4
Anne	8	6	11	6	+3	0
MEAN	5.60	7.40	10.60	5.60	+5.00	−1.80

A close study of the individual essays from the experimental group children shows no consistent pattern of development across the group, but instead isolated experiments in style and structure. Dorothy made the most apparent advance in quality of writing and her later essays combine imagination with control of planning and sentence construction. Compare an extract from 'Adventure while travelling' written before the start of the project with one from the later 'Island Adventure':

> They got out of the helicopter and started walking. They reached a little house which was the image of his own they went in there was a man a girl who was the pilots daughters age and a woman that looked exactly the same as his girls aunt he could not under stand what was happening but he was getting scared he cried for help but there was no help for them. They walked back to the helicopter and it took off he was steering the helicopter when he fell asleep and the helicopter cept flying he woke up in America and he shouted "Hello" to the aunt who was there to meet them. He could not remember any thing of which had happened. (Pre test: Adventure while travelling.)

> When I came out of the water I lay and basked in the lovely hot sun in which I fell asleep. When I woke I saw quite a lot of animals crowding around me. When I stood up they all hurried away I walked down to the forest and started to collect wood and then took it down to the sandy beach. I began to build a small hut in which I could spend some of my time in until I was rescued. That night I was very restless in my small shabby hut so I got up and went to sit beside the blue rippling water. The air was cool and the moon shone brightly and reflected on the water. It was then I could sleep. (Post test: Island adventure.)

For her 'Fairground' essay, Sharon retained the prose–poem style that first appeared in the 'Haunted House' story, but imposed greater order on the structure. The entire essay is given below:

> I can feel my tummy turning as I get nearer the clearing, I can hear the no 1 single blareing in the distance getting nearer and nearer, lights flashing all around blue, red, yellow, green, all flashing at the same time screaming, shouting wild children everywhere playing tig around the many many stalls. Men and women shouting "roll up roll up four balls for 20p try your luck with a goldfish roll up roll up" Old ladies, women, men sitting round in a circle with Boards in front listening to the rapidness of the lady who calls out blue 2 and 1 is 21. over and over. The high seats that go high up in the air you try to touch the sky but never succeed. Then the Ghoust train witch everybody dread to think about, as the the moveing chair starts to get closer to the door you dread to go through then it happens screaming and screeching ghosts bats rats bload skeletons everywhere spider that touch your head a make you scream then the door opens and your out in the open air. But then the men start taking everything down and the park gets quieter and quieter untill theres nobody left but the papers blowing about in the wind and the rubbish left by the people who enjoyed there self so much. yove left it all behind and youll always remember the night at the fair.

The attention shifts from a distant view of the fairground, to the sensations of a traveller in a ghost train. As the pace and involvement heighten, so the sentence constructions alter, from complete sentences, through a sequence of relative clauses, to a welter of words ending in 'make you scream'. Then the activity subsides and the syntax becomes more complex and complete. The final distancing sentence completes the cycle. The language is vibrant and word repetition is used deliberately.

Sharon's 'Island Adventure' is a curious concoction of reflective commentary and stage directions. It has no words or phrases to match those of the Fairground essay, but the essay can be seen as another stage in her experiment with style. The transactional style of the 'Adventure While Travelling' story is replaced by an expressive/poetic style in the 'Haunted House'. Both styles appear in the 'Fairground' essay, though in separate sections, and the merger is taken a step further in the 'Island' story, with transactional statements inserted amongst the expressive/poetic text:

> "It was thursday the 19th, Bengiman Briggs, had just woke up from his rough night at sea, and found that he had been maroonded on an island, Wich island, what island, he did not know." I dont know were to start its all so strange one thing it looks like a deserted island ("but he was wrong") ill go for a swim its to late now for building a shelter. Splash splash splash. oh its lovly ("10 minutes later quite far away from the shore") ahhahhahh a whale splash splash splash ——————— splash knife splodge well least I will have meat for weeks. I better find a bed for the night ill try this path im comeing to forest this should be good for shelter, at last ("it was right at the side of the forest were he found a nice place to sleep").

The sentence construction of James' 'Fairground' essay (written at the end of the teaching scheme) is repetitive and five out of the eleven sentences begin with 'There was' or 'There were'. At word level, the vocabulary is more varied than his earlier descriptive essay and contains some adjective groupings: 'big proud'; 'crowded and overflowing'; 'big, clumsy, dirty'. A considerably more coherent overall structure is found in his 'Island' story, written at the end of the project, than his earlier 'Adventure While Travelling', an extract from which is shown below:

> I ran out the door and over to my friend's house. I got through the window and past there gaurd dog. Then I ran up stairs to wake my friend, then I woke him up. Then we ran to his shed and got our flying saucer that we made, then me and him, took of. Then we destroyed the martians space ship and the in the end we killed the martians. That was the end of my close encounter. Then the day after the martian's invaded earth. They killed humans and destroyed houses and buildings. Me and my friend thought and thought day after night how to kill them. Then we got a chemistry set and made a bacteria. Then

they came to Britain and destroyed London and all the big citie's, Then the came to Edinburgh. We let the the bacteria out of the tube. It killed all the martians and we never heard of them again.

The text of the 'Island Adventure' is bound together by a single theme, cannibals, which is revealed to the reader through a sequence of scenarios — discovery of carcass; boats coming ashore; killing of native man — linked by the subjects' progression round the island:

I then started to make my way through the jungle. After, about two hours walking I came to the end of the jungle, and there I was at the foot of the hill. I said to myself " I have to climb that hill to see if theres any remains from the wereckage of my boat". I started my long journey up the hill at last. I climbed for about 1 hour and I had only got half way up. I looked straight up above me and there I saw some vultures tearing up some kind of carcass. I scrambled up to where the vultures were eating and frightened them away. The remains looked like the arms and legs of a man. I looked under the bushes and there I saw what looked to me like a human skull with some rotting flesh on it. I thought the Island might have been inhabited but the thought faded away quite quickly. After that I climbed to the top and took a look out to sea in the distance I saw tiny black dots come towards the shore. There was native looking people in them. After about half-an-hour, they landed on the shore. It looked like they were lighting a fire and chanting something. Then suddenly I saw them killing a native man with a club. After they had killed him a few of the native men started cutting him up. They must be cannibals I said to myself.

The narrative is linear, with little elaboration, but the gradual development of the theme and the relevance of action to plot (the climbing of the hill both fulfils the stated aim of looking for wreckage of the boat and it provides the author with a setting for the observation of the natives) suggests that the author is building the story to a global plan. The central description is well structured, beginning with a general view — 'I saw some vultures tearing up some kind of carcass' — and then focussing on the remains and the human skull. The inter-sentence links are varied: 3 out of 41 sentences begin with 'then', compared with 8 out of 32 in the 'Adventure while Travelling' story. He includes reflective commentary and, by comparison with the pre essays, the vocabulary, with more groups of modifiers: 'slowly and calmly'; 'tiny black dots'; 'tiny hole of light'.

The text of Louise's 'Island Adventure' story progresses chronologically, with a mixture of simple chain narrative and more complex schemas. Comparison with the 'Adventure while Travelling' story shows some qualitative changes in structure and language at the sentence level: variation in mood and style, and descriptive passages inserted into the narrative. Her 'Fairground' essay, however, shows disappointingly little improvement in style or vocabulary over the 'Visit to the Department' and certainly does not reflect her skills during the project.

Of the control group, only Robert (from a family of avid readers and theatre-goers) appears to have made developments in writing ability comparable to those of Sharon, Dorothy and James. Fears that the project might stunt the children's imagination, or impose unnatural style, were largely unfounded. Clearly, in devoting attention to form, the children sometimes paid too little to content, but their later writings were varied in style and structure and, in the better ones, the writer's personality gleamed through cracks in the mould of the school essay.

7
Future developments

Attitudes towards language and the teaching of writing have changed greatly over the past fifty years. It is no longer accepted that creative writing is a mysterious art, only to be practised by the gifted few. We understand more about the ways and means of teaching writing to children. We have tools that can free words from the printed page and expose the rules and processes that govern language production. In this book, I have attempted to demonstrate that theory, pedagogy and tools can be combined in a computer-based teaching scheme for creative writing. Given the encouraging results of the pilot project, there is good reason to take the ideas further.

The computer programs could be greatly extended. NETTY is the seed of a program that would allow a child to create and explore story plans. WALTER could be developed into a general purpose Writer's Aid, for adults and children, that would lessen the burden of memory and constraint satisfaction, allowing a writer to specify constraints, of style, structure and layout, to the program in a simple text description language. The system would then monitor the text as it was being typed, to ensure the constraints were satisfied. It might perform many of the functions of a proofreader — correcting spelling, tidying headings, references or quotations into a consistent format and indicating repetitions — as well as displaying the layers of text and cross-references between items as a pictorial diagram. The Writer's Aid could be one of a set of 'Tools for Learning', a package of software to help a child to acquire, store and manipulate knowledge, to investigate language, sound and pictures, and to communicate at a distance with other children.

The basic toolkit might include the Writer's Aid, a data collection, calculation and statistics program, a graphics program (with facilities for creating and altering patterns, pictures and graphs), a high-level programming language and an electronic mail system (allowing the user to send and receive written messages via telephone). The computer need not only substitute for conventional class-room equipment such as typewriters, calculators or reference books. It has properties — such as the ability to simulate rule-governed systems, to mimic other machines and to display animated pictures — that could extend the scope and quality of a child's education. New types of educational tools include a package for exploring language, a music synthesiser, an engineering modeller, a dynamics modeller, a map designer and route planner, and a logic programming language. This is obviously only a partial list, other packages could be added, but the choice of a particular item is less important that the general design.

Educational toys already exist, and some have been described in Chapter 4. They are mostly single, independent programs: the word processor cannot incorporate pictures produced by the graphics package; the graphics package cannot display results from the statistics package, and so on. A few attempts have been made to link tools together, but the programs have been slow and difficult to use. This is partly due to the limitations of current educational computers, but also because the enterprise has been seen as joining together individual component programs, rather than creating a single well-integrated system. In the world of business computing multi-purpose computer toolkits are now commonplace and, in the slogan coined by Aaron Sloman (1984): Beginners need powerful systems. Children have as great a range of problems to be solved as research workers or industrialists, but are less skillful in pre-senting their needs clearly and unambiguously, so the computer system must not only offer powerful problem solving and modelling aids, it must also be helpful, tolerant of errors such as spelling mistakes, and capable of explaining its actions.

Such systems are still the stuff of research projects, but a prototype toolkit, written in Logo, was commissioned by the MEP (Microelectronics in Education Programme) Primary Project. Information is created, manipulated and stored entirely as phrasebooks, boxes or Logo turtle commands and the current version of the kit contains modules for data collection and simple statistics, language exploration, transforming geometric shapes, creating and playing Adventure games, and designing one-keypress turtle graphics. Although the individual pro-grams are quite simple, they mesh together (for example, a picture created by the one-keypress Logo can be transformed by the Shapes module or incorpora-ated in the Adventure game) and could act as building blocks for larger systems. At present these programs are designed for use in the classroom, but as home and portable computers become more widespread, they could form part of every child's learning equipment, alongside the pencil, ruler and pocket calculator.

In this vision of educational computing, the computer will not replace or relieve the teacher, nor will it fit neatly into a traditional school curriculum. It will not provide a structured lesson not a well-defined and examinable set of facts. Instead, it will allow a child to become a research worker, with equipment to carry out worthwhile investigations, not only of the physical world but also of thought and language.

Any teaching would come from a human teacher, equipped with written course material. The teaching scheme outlined in this book could be expanded to cover other forms of writing — persuasion, exposition, instruction — other uses of language — speech, literature, drama — and broader cognitive skills, such as problem solving and knowledge representation. To overcome the limitations of current language arts teaching schemes, it would need to provide a sequence of activities from simple structured tasks to open-ended projects, that would take a child from her intuitive awareness of form, pattern and adequacy in language, through the levels of text and components for the writing process to an understanding of the totality of writing as a medium of communication and self-expression.

There is, of course, the question of whether a teaching scheme supported by the latest technology will be any more successful than a sympathetic teacher equipped with pencil, imagination and common sense. A curt response would be that they are not in competition, a competent teacher could draw on the computer and course notes whenever needed, to explain an issue of language or to encourage new writings. But the computer is still a scarce resource and other costly educational innovations, from the Initial Teaching Alphabet to language laboratories, have lain unused, bending the shelves of school storecupboards.

The novel combination of computer and creative writing does need to be assessed, but not through experiments divorced from educational context, nor by using inappropriate tests. In Chapter 3 we showed the limitations of both global impression scores and syntactic indices; a feature analysis supplemented by impressions of the content and integration of the writing may give a fairer indication of short-term developments in writing ability. Feature analysis is certainly more protracted and tiresome than impression marking, but the counting of some features such as unspecific words, word repetition and coordination by 'then' could easily be automated and the automatic detection of others, such as apposition, would make an interesting research project.

The ideal location of a computer-based centre for language exploration and creative writing may not be a conventional classroom. It could be a part of a school library, or in a museum or community centre. It would be stocked with books and audiovisual material as well as computers; children could plan their own study and adults would be available as advisors. This book has provided evidence that children can learn to control and develop their writing abilities in such an environemnt, and enjoy the experience.

Appendix 1

Logo versions of the Phrasebooks, Boxes and Adventure Programs

These programs perform in a similar, but not identical, way to those described in Chapter 5. Both Phrasebooks and Boxes have two levels of operation. They can be operated by commands such as 'teach' and 'do' that provide prompts to guide the user. They also offer commands, such as 'insert' and 'lookmatch' that behave like normal Logo procedures, taking words or lists as input. The appendix contains a user's guide, a summary of commands and a listing for each program. The listings are in Logotron Logo for the BBC B micro, a dialect of Logo that is very similar to Apple Logo for the Apple II micro. A 'Logo pack', with a disk containing these and other toolkit procedures is distributed by MEP Primary Project, St. James Hall, King Alfred's College, Winchester, Hampshire SO22 4NR, England.

THE PHRASEBOOKS TOOL KIT

The PHRASEBOOKS tool kit is a means of representing knowledge in Logo. You can use it, for example, to explore language, to hold a simple conversation with the computer, or to devise a quiz.

PHRASEBOOKS is contained in File PHRASE which must be read into your machine when it is running Logo. There are also some other files which contain example phrasebooks. These files are called FRENCH, GEOG, RANDY, AREA and ELIZA.

(1) To load your PHRASEBOOKS tool kit

When operating normally in Logo at the top level, the computer gives a question mark prompt

?

on the left-hand side of the screen to show that it is ready to receive commands.

There is a choice of modes on the BBC computer, which affect how writing is displayed on the screen, what graphics facilities are available, and how much working memory there is. When you switch into Logo, you are normally in MODE 4, with limited colour graphics available. Using PHRASEBOOK, there is normally no need for any graphics facilities, so the best mode to use is MODE 7. The SETMODE command changes mode. Set up Logo on your machine then type in the commands shown in bold face.

? **SETMODE 7**
? **LOAD "PHRASE**   Wait until the ? prompt is given again,
? **LOAD "FRENCH**   then load the first project file

You can now start using PHRASEBOOKS commands with the phrasebook called FRENCH. It contains a very small English/French dictionary. The commands you can use are

DISPLAY, to look at all the contents of the phrasebook;

FIND, to look up particular phrases in the phrasebook;

TEACH, to add new entries to the phrasebook;

REMOVE, to remove unwanted entries from it;

CONTENTS, to show the contents of the phrasebook after each new entry;

NOCONTENTS, to suppress the printing of the contents.

(2) To use the PHRASEBOOKS

The command FIND is used to look up a particular entry in a phrasebook. It prompts you for the book being used and for the phrase which you want to look up.

? **FIND**

BOOK: **FRENCH**

PHRASE: **DOG**

LE CHIEN

PHRASE: **CAT**

CAT IS NOT IN THE PHRASEBOOK

PHRASE: **HOUSE**

LA MAISON

PHRASE: (*press RETURN*)

?

To finish finding phrases in the phrasebook, press RETURN without typing in anything when given the prompt PHRASE: You will then be returned to top level Logo with the ? prompt.

You can use the command DISPLAY to look at all the contents of the phrasebook FRENCH

? **DISPLAY**
NAME: **FRENCH**

BIG	GRAND	The existing book, including the new
BOOK	LE LIVRE	line will be printed out.
COME	VENIR	
DOG	LE CHIEN	
GO	ALLER	
HOUSE	LA MAISON	
PEN	LE STYLO	
SMALL	PETIT	
TREE	L'ARBRE	

(3) To extend your book

You can add some more entries to your phrasebook with the command TEACH, for instance

WINE	LE VIN
CHILD	L'ENFANT

Make sure that you are at normal top-level Logo operation (shown by the ? prompt), then do the following:

? **TEACH**
BOOK: **FRENCH**

BIG	GRAND	The existing commands in FRENCH will
BOOK	LE LIVRE	then be printed on the screen, followed
COME	VENIR	by the prompt.

DOG	LE CHIEN
GO	ALLER
HOUSE	LA MAISON
PEN	LE STYLO
SMALL	PETIT
TREE	L'ABRE

LEFT PAGE: **WINE**
RIGHT PAGE: **LE VIN**

BIG	GRAND	the existing book, including the
BOOK	LE LIVRE	new line will be printed out
COME	VENIR	
DOG	LE CHIEN	
GO	ALLER	
HOUSE	LA MAISON	
PEN	LE STYLO	
SMALL	PETIT	
TREE	L'ARBRE	
WINE	LE VIN	

LEFT PAGE: **CHILD**
RIGHT PAGE: **L'ENFANT**

BIG	GRAND
BOOK	LE LIVRE
COME	VENIR
DOG	LE CHIEN
GO	ALLER
HOUSE	LA MAISON
PEN	LE STYLO
SMALL	PETIT
TREE	L'ARBRE
WINE	LE VIN
CHILD	L'ENFANT

LEFT PAGE: (*press RETURN*) Press return without typing in anything to leave the procedure TEACH.

You should now be back at the top level of Logo, with the ? prompt. You can try out FIND with the new FRENCH phrasebook, as in section 2.

Printing out the contents of the phrasebook as each new addition is made does take time. If you want to add new entries without showing the contents each time, you can turn off the display by using the command

? **NOCONTENTS**

before using TEACH. Similarly, if later on you want to display the contents each time you make a new addition, then you must use the command

? **CONTENTS**

Both these are top-level Logo commands, so you must exit any procedure you are running (such as TEACH or REMOVE), and get the ? prompt before using them.

(4) To correct mistakes
If you make a mistake with an entry to the book, there are two ways you can correct it.

(a) if the mistake is just in the RIGHT PAGE of an entry, this can be corrected, whilst in TEACH, by retyping that entry correctly. e.g.

? **NOCONTENTS**

? **TEACH**
BOOK: **FRENCH**
LEFT PAGE: **SEA**
RIGHT PAGE: **LA MERE**
LEFT PAGE: **SEA**
RIGHT PAGE: **LA MER**

The book now has LA MER instead of LA MERE as the entry for SEA.

(b) If you have a mistake in the LEFT PAGE of an entry, or want to remove a line altogether from your phrasebook, you must use a different procedure REMOVE.

First press RETURN without typing in anything, in order to leave TEACH. Then

? **REMOVE**
NAME: **FRENCH**
PHRASE: **SEA**   The SEA entry has now been removed.
PHRASE: (*press RETURN*)
?

(5) To write your own phrasebook

You may want to write a completely new phrasebook, e.g. a dictionary in a different language, or an English thesaurus. You can do this in exactly the same way as you extended FRENCH, but you must call the book by another name to distinguish it from FRENCH. Go through section 3 typing in the name of your own book, for example, SPANISH, and add in the words you want after the LEFT PAGE and RIGHT PAGE prompts. To finish adding entries, just press return without typing anything in. This will return you to top level Logo with the ? prompt.

You can write as many books as you like, so long as each one has its own name. Whenever you run FIND you can choose to use any of these books.

Try out your new phrasebooks using FIND again.

(6) To save books

When you have written some books you may want to save them so they can be used another time. Use the standard Logo command SAVE for this. Each book can be saved in a separate data file, which you must name, e.g. if you have created books SPANISH and QUIZ you can save them each in the file with the same name. At the top level type:

? **SAVE "SPANISH ["SPANISH]**
? **SAVE "QUIZ ["QUIZ]**

These are top-level Logo commands and the file name and each of the book-names must be written with a double quote " infront. All the booknames to be saved are enclosed in square brackets. A file name can only have up to 7 letters. You can save more than one book in a file, but this is best avoided, as you can only use one book at a time, and the book you are not using will fill up space in the computer, once the file has been loaded.

Another time, to run PHRASEBOOKS using one of these books you must load the data file immediately after loading the PHRASE file.

? **LOAD "PHRASE**
? **LOAD "SPANISH**

(7) Suggestions for projects

The dictionary file given here is very small, as it is just a sample to illustrate its use. You can develop quite extensive dictionaries in the same way. The left page of the book does not have to be just a single word, so you could include common phrases as well as single words, e.g.

WHAT IS YOUR NAME   COMMENT VOUZ APPELEZ VOUS

You could also develop a thesaurus for children to use. This would have single word entries on the LEFT PAGE, and a choice of alternative synonyms on the RIGHT PAGE, e.g.

> ? **TEACH**
> BOOK: **THESAURUS**
> LEFT PAGE: **PRETTY**
> RIGHT PAGE: **BEAUTIFUL, ATTRACTIVE, CHARMING, PLEASANT**
> LEFT PAGE: **BIG**
> RIGHT PAGE: **HUGE, TALL, ENORMOUS, LARGE, GREAT**
> etc.

(8) Pattern matching

There is a pattern matching facility built in to the phrasebooks, which gives far greater possibilities than first appear.

The book GEOGRAPHY, contained in the file GEOG, is a mini database on the geography of the British Isles. Try out the examples below.

> ? **ER OPNS**   A standard Logo command that clears
> ? **LOAD "GEOG**   out the existing phrasebooks.
> ? **FIND**
> BOOK: **GEOGRAPHY**
> PHRASE: **WHICH RIVER FLOWS THROUGH MANCHESTER**
> MERSEY
> PHRASE:

Try out each of the following, and also use your own wording.

ON WHICH RIVER IS GLASGOW BUILT
WHAT IS THE NAME OF THE RIVER WHICH RUNS THROUGH
    OXFORD

The pattern matching facility allows the key words 'RIVER' and 'MANCHESTER' to be recognised within a natural English sentence. Use DISPLAY to show the contents of GEOGRAPHY. Question marks match a word or words in the phrase to be looked up. A single question mark ?, matches with a single word and double question marks ?? match with any number of words from zero upwards. Thus the phrase

WHICH RIVER FLOWS THROUGH MANCHESTER

matches with the LEFT PAGE

>>?? RIVER ?? MANCHESTER ??

However, the sentence

>MANCHESTER IS ON WHAT RIVER

will not match, as the key words, MANCHESTER and RIVER, are in the wrong order. If you wanted to match this sentence as well, you would have to add a new line to the phrasebook, using TEACH:

>LEFT PAGE: **?? MANCHESTER ?? RIVER ??**

>RIGHT PAGE: **MERSEY**

You can extend this idea in any way you want, e.g. the capital cities of Europe. where the key words would be CAPITAL and the name of the country.

(9) Logo commands

You can use your phrasebooks to give instructions to carry out normal Logo commands, such as turtle commands, or arithmetic calculations. If the RIGHT PAGE begins with a Logo command, such as PRINT or FD then the right hand side is not printed out, but is run like a Logo command at top level. Thus you can create a one keypress Logo with entries like:

>F   FORWARD 100
>R   RIGHT 90

The book RANDY, contained in a file of the same name, recognises key turtle commands and moves the turtle with a random input. To use this, you will need to be in mode 4, for turtle graphics. To change modes you must clear the workspace and reload PHRASE.

>? **ERALL**   To clear the workspace
>? **SETMODE 4**
>? **LOAD "PHRASE**
>? **LOAD "RANDY**
>? **FIND**
>BOOK: **RANDY**
>PHRASE:

Try out some of these and make up your own commands too.

>GO FORWARD
>TURN ROUND
>TURN A BIT MORE
>GO BACK A BIT
>GO LEFT
>TURN RIGHT

When you have finished using FIND, have a look at the book RANDY using DISPLAY. You will see that the same key word system is used as for GEOGRAPHY, but the right page in each case is now a turtle command.

You can write similar phrasebooks to carry out simple Logo commands, using a special pass word, for example, or recognising 'a little' and 'a lot' to determine how far the turtle moves, or to draw set shapes, e.g.

DRAW A SQUARE
DRAW A LARGE TRIANGLE

(10) Bugs and debugging

If a phrasebook you have written is not working in the way you expect, check that you have put the first word of any commands on the RIGHT PAGE into RUNNABLE?. (See Section 11 below).

There may be a problem with question marks, or full stops put at the end of a question. e.g. in GEOGRAPHY if the following are typed in at the keyboard:

ON WHICH RIVER IS BRISTOL BUILT?

WHICH RIVER GOES THROUGH DURHAM?

The first will get the reply AVON, but the second will get an error message. As the phrasebook stands, Durham is recognised, but Durham? is not. The phrasebook could be changed to recognise either version. Otherwise it may be easier to miss out punctuation at the end of every sentence.

(11) Running Logo procedures

When using a phrasebook to run a Logo procedure, e.g. giving turtle commands, or evaluating arithmetic expressions, the particular commands used must be recognised. The procedure RUNNABLE? contains a list of Logo commands that are recognised as the first thing on the right-hand page:

```
TO RUNNABLE?  : ITEM
     OP MEMBER?  : ITEM [PRINT SHOW RANDOM FD BK LT RT]
END
```

In the AREA example the command PRINT is used to print out the answers. In RANDY only the commands FD, BK, LT or RT are used, with RANDOM. You might want to extend this range of commands, to include HOME, CLEAR-SCREEN, etc. This is quite possible, as long as RUNNABLE? is edited to include any commands used on the RIGHT PAGE of the phrasebook.

(12) More pattern matching: using variables

The examples above used the symbols ? and ?? inside phrasebooks to match with any words. e.g.

?? CAPITAL ?? ENGLAND

would match with

WHAT IS THE CAPITAL CITY OF ENGLAND
WHICH CITY IS THE CAPITAL OF ENGLAND

There are two more examples of phrasebooks given in the files AREA and ELIZA. The book name and the file name are the same in each case.

PROJECT 1. AREA

Go through the instructions given in section 8 for loading an example phrase-book, and then use FIND on the book AREA. This book allows you to ask arithmetic questions in natural language and gives the answers.

Try the phrases

WHAT IS THE AREA OF A SQUARE OF SIDE 19
TELL ME THE AREA OF A CIRCLE OF RADIUS 14 CMS
WHAT IS THE AREA OF A TRIANGLE OF BASE 12 AND HEIGHT 20

Use DISPLAY to look at the phrasebook, and use TEACH to add some entries of your own to it. You will see that the numbers used are represented by variables, ?X and ?Y. In the matching process, say for the first phrase,

WHAT IS THE AREA OF A SQUARE OF SIDE 19

is matched to the left page entry

?? AREA OF A SQUARE OF SIDE ?X ??

?X then takes on the value 19. The right page is then worked out and printed using this value.

PRINT ?X * ?X

As with the ? and ?? symbols, ?X stands for one word or number, and ??X stands for any quantity of numbers or words, including zero.

PROJECT 2. ELIZA

In 1969, Joe Weizenbaum wrote a program called Eliza. It was the first program that could hold a free-ranging conversation in normal English language. He designed it to simulate a psychotherapist, encouraging a patient to talk, and giving non-directive replies. At the time it was the centre of a great controversy with some researchers seriously suggesting that computers should replace human psychiatrists. The ELIZA program in fact knew nothing about any person's mental health. It worked purely by matching patterns of words. The following 'conversation' was obtained using FIND with a simple phrasebooks version of ELIZA held in the file ELIZA.

```
?  ER OPNS
?  LOAD "ELIZA
?  FIND
BOOK; ELIZA
```

PHRASE: **DO YOU LOVE ME**

WOULD YOU LIKE ME TO LOVE YOU

PHRASE: **I THINK YOU ARE NICE**

WHY DO YOU THINK THAT I AM NICE

PHRASE: **MY MOTHER HATES ME**

TELL ME MORE ABOUT YOUR FAMILY

PHRASE: **YOU ARE SO UNDERSTANDING**

WHY DO YOU THINK I AM SO UNDERSTANDING

This is a very limited version with plenty of room for improvement, modification and development.

Level 2 — Logo Procedures

You may wish to include the phrasebooks procedures in one of your own programs, for instance to access a database using natural language. There are two Logo procedures to do this: INSERT and LOOKMATCH. INSERT takes three lists as inputs' the left and right page entries to be added, and the book. It outputs the amended version of the book:

MAKE "MYBOOK INSERTS [CAT] [LE CHAT] [ ]
MAKE "MYBOOK INSERT [DOG] [LE CHIEN] : MYBOOK

LOOKMATCH takes two lists as inputs, the pattern to be matched and the book. It outputs the right page of the matched entry:

PRINT LOOKMATCH [CAT] : MYBOOK

The procedure FOREVER takes one input, a list of commands, and repeats these commands until ESCAPE is pressed. RL reads a list typed in by the user. It can be used with FOREVER and LOOKMATCH to create a quiz or conversation; e.g.:

FOREVER [PRINT LOOKMATCH RL : MYBOOK]

BOXES TOOL KIT

You can use BOXES, for a wide range of different applications. The idea of a BOX is that it contains several unordered items, any of which can be pulled out, at random. Boxes can contain single words, phrases, sentences or word patterns (which include the names of other boxes). The tool kit described in this section shows one application: generating sentences. The kit is contained in the file BOXES, which must be read in after loading Logo. It contains some of the same procedures as PHRASEBOOKS, such as DISPLAY and REMOVE, but the commands for entering data into boxes and using the contents of the boxes are different. The command.

PUT

puts new data into a box. The two commands

DO
LOTS

generate words and sentences. There are two demonstration files of boxes. The file FARM contains a demonstration that generates random sentences, and HAIKU has boxes to generate Haiku poems.

(1) To load the boxes tool kit

? **LOAD "BOXES**
? **LOAD "FARM**

You can use the DO command to ask boxes to generate an example of the pattern you specify (in this case a sentence).

> ? **DO**
> WORD PATTERN: **SENTENCE**
>
> THE SILLY WOMABAT EATS THE HAIRY DONKEY
>
> WORD PATTERN: **SENTENCE BUT SENTENCE**
>
> THE HAIRY WOMBAT LIKES THE SPOTTED DOG BUT THE SILLY DONKEY EATS THE WOMBAT
>
> WORD PATTERN: (*press RETURN*)
> ?

Press RETURN to leave the procedure DO.

What happens is this: DO reads each word in the pattern in turn. If this word is not the name of a box (like BUT) then it is just printed out. If it is a box name, then DO generates an example at random from that box. As words are generated at random from boxes, you are likely to get different sentences to the ones given here, when you try it out.

If you want to generate lots of sentences on the same pattern, you can use LOTS in place of DO. The sentence generation continues until you press RETURN.

> ? **LOTS**
> WORD PATTERN: **SENTENCE**
>
> THE DOG DEVOURS THE WOMBAT
> THE HAIRY WOMBAT EATS THE SPOTTED WOMBAT
> THE SPOTTED DOG LIKES THE SILLY WOMBAT
> THE WOMBAT TICKLES THE HAIRY DONKEY

To look at the contents of any of the boxes you can use DISPLAY. Try it out on the box SENTENCE.

> ? **DISPLAY**
> NAME: **SENTENCE**
> NOUNPHRASE VERB NOUNPHRASE
> ?

Sentence contains only one item. This is a list of three other boxes, NOUNPHRASE, VERB and NOUNPHRASE, i.e. to generate a sentence DO first generates a nounphrase, followed by a verb, followed by a nounphrase. Use DISPLAY on these boxes to find out what they contain.

> ? **DISPLAY**
> NAME: **NOUNPHRASE**
> THE NOUN
> THE ADJECTIVE NOUN
> ?

Nounphrase has two items, THE NOUN, and THE ADJECTIVE NOUN. They indicate that a nounphrase can be either the word 'THE' followed by a 'NOUN', (e.g. THE DONKEY) or 'THE' followed by an 'ADJECTIVE' followed by a 'NOUN' (e.g. THE HAIRY WOMBAT). NOUN and ADJECTIVE are also boxes which you can display in the same way.

The complete rules of the grammar in this file are these (Box names are given in capital letters).

— SENTENCE — is a NOUNPHRASE followed by a VERB, followed by a
    NOUNPHRASE
— NOUNPHRASE — is either 'The NOUN' or 'The ADJECTIVE NOUN'
— NOUN — is DONKEY, WOMBAT or DOG
— VERB — is EATS, DEVOURS, LIKES or TICKLES;
— ADJECTIVE — is HAIRY, SPOTTED or SILLY

This is by no means a complete grammar. It just gives you some language parts to explore and extend.

The box named BOXES contains the names of all the boxes, so to find out which ones have been created type:

? **DISPLAY**
NAME: **BOXES**

SENTENCE
NOUNPHRASE
VERB
NOUN
ADJECTIVE

(2) Extending boxes

You can use the procedure PUT to make new boxes, or to put new words into existing boxes. Add some words of your own to the existing NOUN, VERB and ADJECTIVE boxes, then try generating more sentences.

? **PUT**
BOX NAME: **NOUN**   Add your own word to the ITEM prompt.
WOMBAT
DONKEY
DOG

ITEM: **OTTER**
WOMBAT
DONKEY
DOG
OTTER

ITEM: **ELEPHANT**
WOMBAT
DONKEY
DOG
OTTER
ELEPHANT

ITEM: (*press RETURN*)
?

To leave the procedure, press RETURN at the ITEM prompt.

As with the PHRASEBOOKS, if you do not want the contents of the box printed out each time you make a new entry in it, you can switch off the display with the command

? **NOCONTENTS**

You must first be at top-level Logo, with the ? prompt. If you are in a procedure, e.g. PUT, you must first leave the procedure, by pressing RETURN. You can then type NOCONTENTS and then, if required, return to the procedure by typing PUT. If you want the contents displayed again later on, use the command

? **CONTENTS**

to switch it on when you are at top level Logo.

Use PUT to add more words to each of the boxes, then try generating more sentences with DO and LOTS.

You can extend not only the lists of words but also the word patterns. Try adding a new pattern to NOUNPHRASE, e.g. the NOUN in the PLACE.

? **PUT**
BOX NAME: **NOUNPHRASE**

THE NOUN
THE ADJECTIVE NOUN

ITEM: **THE NOUN IN THE PLACE**

THE NOUN
THE ADJECTIVE NOUN
THE NOUN IN THE PLACE

ITEM: (*press RETURN*)

You then need to use PUT to create a new box called PLACE with contents like FARMYARD, KITCHEN, PUDDLE, etc.

(3) Correcting mistakes

If you make a mistake in typing in the contents of a box, you can remove an entry using the command REMOVE. Again this command can only be used when you are at the top level of Logo.

? **NOCONTENTS**
? **PUT**
BOX NAME: **NOUN**
ITEM: **ELECTRICIAN**
ITEM: **CAT**
ITEM: **JUMP**
ITEM: (*press return*)

```
?  REMOVE
NAME:  NOUN
ITEM:   JUMP
ITEM:  (press return)
?  PUT
BOX NAME:
```

Continue adding items to boxes.

If you remove all the contents of one particular box, then the box itself will be removed. Also if you want to remove a whole box and contents, you can do this by removing the box name from a special box named BOXES which holds the names of every box.

```
?  REMOVE
NAME:  BOXES

ANIMAL
PLACE
VERB
ADJECTIVE
ADVERB
NOUN
NOUNPHRASE
SENTENCE

ITEM: PLACE

ANIMAL
VERB
ADJECTIVE
ADVERB
NOUN
NOUNPHRASE
SENTENCE
ITEM: (press RETURN)
```

(4) Suggestions for projects

(a) You can make boxes of your own in exactly the same way that you added contents to other boxes. Each box must have its own name. These can then be used in sentence generation patterns to suit your own purposes. For instance, you can generate your own game of consequences with boxes MAN, WOMEN, SITUATION, SPOKE and RESULT. The word patterns would then be as follows, with box names given in capital letters.

MAN met WOMAN SITUATION.
He said SPOKE
She said SPOKE
RESULT.

(b) You can change the sort of sentence patterns you use, to generate poetry, short rhymes and limericks.

There once was NOUNPHRASE from PLACE1
Whose NOUN was an awful RHYME1

You could write different boxes of rhyming words.

(c) The file called HAIKU contains boxes to generate Haiku. This is a form of Japanese poetry, which always has three lines and is about nature and seasons. (It should also have a total of 17 syllables, but we have ignored that restriction.)

>   **LOAD "HAIKU**
>   **DO**

WORD PATTERN: **HAIKU**

TIMID WARM CLOUD SHIMMERS
FRAGRANT EAGLE RISES AND
STARTLES THE TIMID CLOUD

Investigate how the poetry is produced, by looking at the boxes used in generating it. Then add your own vocabullary and try to write your own Haiku on any theme you want. You could also try creating Haiku of exactly 17 syllables, by creating separate boxes of one-syllable words, two-syllable words, etc. and using an appropriate word pattern.

(5) Other uses for boxes

(a) Although the examples used so far are all of sentence generation, boxes are in fact flexible tools which can be used in a wide range of applications. The contents of the boxes do not have to be words; they can be musical notes or turtle commands, for instance. You can build boxes to draw random patterns:

>   **PUT**

BOX NAME: **MOVE**
ITEM: **FD 50**
ITEM: **BK 120**
ITEM: **FD 20**
ITEM: **FD 100**
ITEM: (*press RETURN*)

>   **PUT**

BOX NAME: **TURN**
ITEM: **RT 30**
ITEM: **RT 120**
ITEM: **LT 50**
ITEM: **LT 90**
ITEM: (*press RETURN*)

>   **PUT**

BOX NAME: **TURTLE**
ITEM: **MOVE MOVE TURN**
ITEM: **MOVE TURN**
ITEM: **TURN MOVE**
ITEM: (*press RETURN*)

? **LOTS**
WORD PATTERN: **TURTLE**

If the words generated by boxes are Logo commands then these commands are run. The list of commands is in the procedure RUNNABLE? (See Phrasebooks section 11). Any new commands contained in a box must be included in RUNNABLE? in order for them to be run.

(b) You can write interactive poetry, where the poem prompts you for a word, and then uses it. This is done by preceding the word with a # sign, for example, #WHATEVER. When this occurs in a word pattern, the computer gives a prompt WHATEVER? It accepts anything typed in at that point and also adds it to the box WHATEVER, e.g.

? **DO**
WORD PATTERN: **#NAME lives in PLACE with a pet #ANIMAL**

NAME? **MR BLOGGS**

ANIMAL? **COCKROACH**

MR BLOGGS LIVES IN A TIN HUT WITH A PET COCKROACH
?

If you just press RETURN instead of typing anything in when given the prompt NAME? then DO takes an item at random out of the NAME box instead.

Level 2 – Logo Procedures
You may want to incorporate procedures to create or generate from boxes as part of your own programs. There are two procedures for this, INBOX and SCAN. INBOX adds a new item to a box. It takes two list inputs, one for the item and one containing the current contents of the box, e.g.

MAKE "ANIMAL INBOX [LION] [ ]

MAKE "ANIMAL INBOX [ORANG UTANG] :ANIMAL

This can be used in place of PUT. SCAN takes one input, a list containing the word pattern, e.g.

PRINT SCAN [THE ANGRY ANIMAL]

THE ANGRY LION

It generates words according to the pattern. The procedure FOREVER takes one input, a list of commands, and repeats these commands until ESCAPE is pressed. It can be used with SCAN to generate words repeatedly.

FOREVER [PRINT SCAN [THE ADJECTIVE ANIMAL]]

ADVENTURE TOOL KIT

(1) Introduction
ADVENTURE is a small example of the type of adventure program which can be generated with the aid of the Logo tool kit. You can play the adventure as it stands; at a later stage you can modify its contents or even extend it further.

(2) Operating instructions for ADVENTURE

Before you do anything else you should make a backup of the ADVENTURE disk, because ADVENTURE overwrites the disk each time you make a move. In order to do the backup you will need a blank, initialised disk. Use the *ENABLE and *BACKUP commands to copy the disk.

Set up Logo on your machine, insert the Tool kit disk and then type in the bold face commands, pressing RETURN after each one.

    ? **SETMODE 7**
    ? **LOAD "PHRASE**
    ? **LOAD "BOXES**

> Remove the Logo Tool kit disk and replace it with the ADVENTURE disk.

    ? **LOAD "ADVENT**

    ? **ADVENTURE**   To start playing the adventure.

(3) Playing the Adventure

The adventure begins with the following description

> YOU ARE STANDING ON A BEACH
> TO THE SOUTH OF A STEEP HILL.
> A PATH LEADS WEST.
>
> YOU CAN SEE:
>
> BOX OF MATCHES
>
> WHAT DO YOU WANT TO DO?

Decide what you want to do. The goal of this adventure is to find some elvish gold and bring it back to the beach. You can pick up anything you find by typing a suitable command. You may want to take the box of matches or you might want to follow the path. Simply type in your wishes in plain English and the press RETURN, e.g.

> WHAT DO YOU WANT TO DO? **GO WEST**

If the program does not seem to understand you, then try re-wording your wishes. Finding out the wording which works is very much an integral part of solving most computer adventures. If you forget what you are carrying you can check by typing: WHAT AM I CARRYING Always wait for the prompt WHAT DO YOU WANT TO DO? before typing in more instructions.

If you don't type in any instructions but simply press RETURN, this is interpreted as a wish to leave the ADVENTURE program and return to Logo. The adventure will be saved on the disk and you will then see the following message on the screen.

> GAME FINISHED. TO RESTART IT
> TYPE: EXPLORE "HILL

Note that the name of the location, e.g. HILL, will be the one you were at when the adventure ended. If restart the adventure you will find that you are carrying all the objects you picked up before. If you want to resume the game some other time just load "PHRASE and "BOXES then put in the old disk and load "AD-VENT. Then type EXPLORE followed by the last location you visited, e.g. EXOLORE "HILL.

(5) Extending your adventure

You might want to create new locations in the adventure. You can do this quite easily providing you are familiar with the PHRASEBOOK and BOXES parts of the Logo Tool Kit. Let's suppose you think it might be nice to have something more exciting happen if players choose to go south from the beach. Here is how to do it. Finish the game at any location (or if you are starting from scratch then load the "PHRASE, "BOXES and "ADVENT as described earlier). Next, make sure that your new location does not already exist by typing:

   ? **DISPLAY**
   NAME: **PLACES**

You will then be shown a list of all the locations in the adventures as it exists at present. These should be:

   BEACH, HILL, FOREST, FOREST1, FOREST2, CAVE, HILL and HALL

We can see that it will be perfectly safe to call our new location SEA, so type:

   ? **CREATE**
   PLACE NAME: **SEA**

The Logo edit screen will be shown. Type in the Logo commands which will be run to provide the descriptions you want displayed when anyone reaches the sea.

Here is an example:

```
TO SEA
PR [YOU STAND IN THE SEA.]
PR [THE WAVES BREAK AGAINST YOUR KNOBBLY KNEES.]
PR [FAR TO THE SOUTH THERE IS AN ISLAND.]
END
```

When you are satisfied with your description hold down CONTROL and press C. You will see the following message:

SEA DEFINED
ADD THE COMMANDS TO MOVE FROM THE SEA
LEFT PAGE:

As you may guess, you are using the PHRASEBOOK to add the commands. The phrase from the player's instructions which you want the program to match goes on the left page, and the effect you want it to have goes on the right page. For example we know that if players want to go north, they should be returned to the beach. So for the left page type ?? NORTH ?? and press RETURN. For the matching right page type BEACH and press RETURN. On the other hand they might elect to try their luck to the south where that island lies. So for the left hand page type ?? SOUTH ?? and for the matching right page type ISLAND. Let's suppose you want them to come to a sticky end if they choose to go east. Type ?? EAST ?? for the left page and KILLED for the right page. If they choose to go west, let's give them a grim message and leave them where they are. Type ?? WEST ?? for the left page and MORTALS MAY NOT PASS THIS WAY for the right page.

The phrasebook should now look like this:

?? NORTH ??	BEACH
?? SOUTH ??	ISLAND
?? EAST ??	KILLED
?? WEST ??	MORTALS MAY NOT PASS THIS WAY

Note that a single word on the right-hand page is an instruction to move to that location, and more than one word means it is a message to be shown the player, and the location remains unchanged.

Assuming that this is all the choices we are going to allow, press RETURN on its own. You will next see the message:

NOW ADD THE ITEMS TO BE FOUND AT SEA

If you don't want anything just press RETURN. But let's assume we want them to see a bottle.

ITEM: **FLOATING BOTTLE**
ITEM:

If there is nothing else to add, press RETURN and the new location will be saved on the disk.

A number of additional actions have to be taken before the adventure is ready to be played. First of all you will have to create that ISLAND location. Next you need to be aware of the KILLED option. This is a built-in feature of the adventure as it stands. Wherever it is invoked, it has the effect of displaying the message 'Oops, you have got yourself killed.' and ending the adventure. Lastly, we have to make sure that our new SEA location links up with the existing adventure. At the moment it does not. The logical place to make the link is inside the BEACH location.

?   **CREATE**
PLACE NAME: **BEACH**

This will bring the BEACH procedure into the Logo editor. We need to tempt the players into the sea, so insert the following line.

PR [BEHIND YOU LIES THE SOUTH SEA]

Then define the procedure by holding down CONTROL and pressing C. Beach will be defined and you will see the message:

ADD THE COMMANDS TO MOVE FROM THE BEACH

Below this will appear all the left and right-hand pages associated with the location. They should look like this:

```
?? CLIMB ?? HILL ??    HILL
?? NORTH ??            HILL
?? WEST ??             FOREST
?? SOUTH ??            KILLED
?? EAST ??             YOU ARE STOPPED BY A SHEER CLIFF
?? GO UP ??            HILL
```

If you look you will see that ?? SOUTH ?? is paired with KILLED. This will need to be changed. For the left page type ?? SOUTH ?? and for the right page type SEA. After this press RETURN on its own and you should see the message:

NOW ADD ITEMS TO BE FOUND AT BEACH

    BOX OF MATCHES

You won't want to change this, so just press RETURN; the amended BEACH location will be saved to disk.

(6) Writing a new adventure

Before doing this it is best to plan your adventure on paper. Draw a sketch of all the locations. Decide how they interconnect. Make up your mind about hazards and objects which may be found. Have a clear idea about where the adventure will start.

First make a fresh copy of the ADVENTURE disk. Load in the adventure in the usual way, then type:

? **MAKE "PLACES [ ]**   This clears the list of locations recognised by the program.

? **CREATE**

Follow the procedures for creating locations. Note that the first location you create will be the one at which the adventure will always start.

(7) More advanced adventures

It is possible to introduce complex features like magical talismans and like into your adventure, provided that you understand the conditional structure set out below. Basically you need to decide what power certain objects have and then make some of the actions conditional on their being carried by the adventurer. These examples should help you:

Suppose that we are creating a location from which escape is only possible if the adventurer is carrying certain objects.

Assume that you have loaded in the "PHRASE, "BOXES and "ADVENT procedures in the usual way. Type:

? **CREATE**
PLACE NAME: **TRAP**

First of all type in the description, when it is finished it might look like this:

TO TRAP
PR [YOU ARE IN A TRAP]
PR [ABOVE YOU CAN SEE THE STARS]
PR [TO THE SOUTH IS A LITTLE OAK DOOR]
PR [ ]
PR [A MINE-SHAFT YAWNS AT YOUR FEET]

IF HOLDING? [[BLACK MARBLE]] [PR [THE LADDER RUNGS LOOK ROTTEN] [PR [A STURDY LADDER LEADS DOWN]]

The last line means:

> IF the adventurer is HOLDING the BLACK MARBLE give the warning about the rotten ladder rungs, but if the adventurer does not have the marble then say that the ladder looks strong.

Note: the placing and number of brackets is very important.

Define the procedure in the usual way.

Now let's allow only three directions of travel. If they choose to go down and they are holding the black stone, they will be killed. If they are not holding it they will reach the mine. If they choose to go up and are holding the rope they will move to the meadow. Finally, if they choose to go south and they are holding the ring and the rabbit, they will come to the palace. If the adventurers do not carry these items, take them to the dungeon.

After you see the message telling you to:

ADD THE COMMANDS TO MOVE FROM THE TRAP

type in the left and right-hand pages in the usual way. The result should look like this:

?? DOWN ??	IF HOLDING? [[BLACK STONE]] [[KILLED PR [THE LADDER BROKE AND YOU FELL.]]] [[MINE]]
?? UP ??	IF HOLDING? [[ROPE]] [[MEADOW]] [[TRAP PR [TOO DIFFICULT TO CLIMB]]]
?? SOUTH ??	IF HOLDING? [[RING] [RABBIT]] [[PALACE]] [[DUNGEON PR [NO RING NO RABBIT NO FREEDOM]]]

We won't need any items to be found in the TRAP so pressing RETURN successively will save this location to disk.

By now you should be able to see the general pattern of things; the last line of instructions translates as:

> When adventurers choose to go SOUTH, IF they are HOLDING the RING and the RABBIT, then move to the PALACE. If the adventurers have

neither item, or only one, then go to the DUNGEON and display a message with a hint in it.

(8) For the really adventurous

There are many other ways of creating more complex effects. To do this you will need to look at the locations contained in the `ADVENT` file. Telling you how to do this would be contrary to the spirit of both adventure games and Logo. So it is up to you.

PROCEDURES USED IN THE TOOL KITS

(1) Procedures used in the PHRASEBOOKS tool kit

CONTENTS — Switches on the display of contents of the current book, when using TEACH or REMOVE. As each item is added to, or taken from the book, the complete contents are printed out. It is cancelled by the command NO-CONTENTS.

DISPLAY — Displays the contents of a phrasebook or box (or any other data structure in other tool kits). It gives a prompt for the name of the book or box.

FIND — Looks up any particular entry in a phrasebook. It prompts for the bookname and the phrase, which is the left page of the entry. It prints out the contents of the right page.

NOCONTENTS — Switches off the display of contents in TEACH or REMOVE (see CONTENTS).

REMOVE — Removes one or more lines from a phrasebook. It gives prompts for the bookname and the line to be removed, and prints out the current contents of the book, (unless NOCONTENTS has been used).

TEACH — Enters items into a phrasebook. It gives prompts for the name of the book, and the entry on the left page and the right page. The bookname must be a single word. The current contents of the book are printed out after each new entry is made, unless NOCONTENTS has been used.

PHRASEBOOKS: Level 2

INSERT :LEFT PAGE :RIGHT PAGE :BOOK — Can be used to add new entries to a book directly. It takes three lists as inputs; the left and right page entries which are to be added, and the book name. It ouputs the amended version of the book.

    MAKE "BOOK INSERT [CAT] [LE CHAT] [ ]

LOOKMATCH :LEFTPAGE :BOOK — This takes two lists as inputs, the pattern to be matched and the book. It returns the right page of the matched entry.

    PRINT LOOKMATCH [CAT] :BOOK

RUNNABLE? :ITEM — This is a test of whether a command is recognised. It takes a word as input. Any Logo primitive or procedure, when used as the first item on the right page of a phrasebook, can be run directly, if it is recognised. If you want to run new procedures through a phrasebook, the name of the procedure must be added to the list in line one of RUNNABLE?.

(2) Procedures used in the BOXES tool kit

DISPLAY — This is used to display the contents of a box. It gives a prompt for the name of the box.

REMOVE — Removes one or more items from a box. It gives prompts for the box name and the item to be removed, and prints out the current contents of the box. If all the contents of a box are removed, then the box too is removed. If you want to take out a complete box and all its contents, you do this by using REMOVE on the boxname in the box named BOXES.

CONTENTS — Switches on the display of contents of a box, when using PUT or REMOVE. As each item is added to or taken from the box, the complete contents are printed out.

NOCONTENTS — Switches off the display of contents in PUT or REMOVE.

PUT — Enters items into a new or existing box. It prompts for the box name and the item, and (if NOCONTENTS has not been used) prints out the current state of the box at each new addition.

DO — Generates a sentence from a word pattern, by picking at random words from any of the boxes specified in the pattern. Any words used in the pattern, which are not box names, are simply printed out. The procedure gives a prompt for the word pattern.

LOTS — This is similar to DO, but instead of generating one example, it will continue to generate sentences on the given pattern until RETURN is pressed. It also prompts for the word pattern.

BOXES — Level 2

INBOX :ITEM :NAME — Takes two inputs, an item and a box name. If the item is not already in the box, it puts it in.

MAKE "PLACE INBOX [KITCHEN] [ ]

SCAN :PATTERN — Generates random elements from boxes, when given a pattern containing box names.

PRINT SCAN [THE ANIMAL]

RUNNABLE? :ITEM — Checks if an item from a box is a recognised Logo command which can be run. Procedures and commands for generating music or turtle graphics must be included in the first line of RUNNABLE? in order for them to operate properly.

Procedures used in the ADVENTURE tool kit

ADVENTURE — Runs the adventure game.

CREATE — To extend the game. It gives prompts for the location and then asks for the procedure that will be run on entering the location, the phrasebook of move commands and the box of items at that location.

Contents of the file PHRASE

```
TO TEACH
PRINT "
MAKE ".BOOKNAME .ASK_FOR_NAME [BOOK]
IF EMPTY? :.BOOKNAME [STOP]
IF NOT NAME? :.BOOKNAME [MAKE :.BOOKNAME []]
IF NOT NAME? ".DISPLAYOK [MAKE ".DISPLAYOK TRUE]
.TEACHBIT :.BOOKNAME :.DISPLAYOK
END


TO FIND
PRINT "
MAKE ".BOOKNAME .ASK_FOR_NAME [BOOK]
IF EMPTY? :.BOOKNAME [PRINT " STOP]
IF NOT NAME? :.BOOKNAME [PRINT [OOPS - THERE IS NO BOOK NAMED]
   PRINT :.BOOKNAME FIND STOP]
PRINT "
.FINDBIT :.BOOKNAME
END

TO CONTENTS
MAKE ".DISPLAYOK TRUE
END

TO NOCONTENTS
MAKE ".DISPLAYOK FALSE
END

TO REMOVE
PRINT "
MAKE ".NAME .ASK_FOR_NAME [NAME]
PRINT "
IF EMPTY? :.NAME [STOP]
IF NOT NAME? :.NAME
   [PRINT [OOPS - THERE IS NO BOX OR BOOK NAMED] PRINT :.NAME PRINT " STOP]
IF WORD? FIRST FIRST THING :.NAME [.REMOVE_BOX :.NAME] [.REMOVE_BOOK :.NAME]
PRINT "
END

TO DISPLAY
PRINT "
MAKE ".NAME .ASK_FOR_NAME [NAME]
PRINT "
IF EMPTY? :.NAME [STOP]
IF NOT NAME? :.NAME [PRINT [OOPS - THERE IS NO BOX OR BOOK NAMED]
   PRINT :.NAME PRINT " STOP]
IF WORD? FIRST THING :.NAME [PRINT THING :.NAME PRINT " STOP]
IF WORD? FIRST FIRST THING :.NAME [.DISPLAY_BOX THING :.NAME]
   [.DISPLAY_BOOK THING :.NAME]
PRINT "
END

TO INSERT :.LP :.RP :.BOOK
IF EMPTY? :.BOOK [OP LPUT LIST :.LP :.RP []]
IF EQUAL? :.LP FIRST FIRST :.BOOK [OP FPUT LIST :.LP :.RP BF :.BOOK]
   [OP FPUT FIRST :.BOOK INSERT :.LP :.RP BF :.BOOK]
END
```

```
TO LOOKMATCH :ENTRY :BOOK
MAKE ".ASSIGNED FALSE
IF EMPTY? :BOOK [OP []]
IF WORD? :ENTRY [MAKE "ENTRY FPUT :ENTRY []]
IF NOT .MATCHES? :ENTRY FIRST FIRST :BOOK [OP LOOKMATCH :ENTRY BF :BOOK]
IF :.ASSIGNED [OP .FILL LAST FIRST :BOOK] [OP LAST FIRST :BOOK]
END

TO RUNNABLE? :WORD
OP MEMBER? :WORD [PR PRINT SHOW TYPE RUN REPEAT TOPLEVEL CLEAN CT CS
    HOME HT PD PU ST FD FORWARD BK BACK LEFT LT RIGHT RT SETBG SETC SETH SETPC
    SETPOS SETX SETY]
END

TO FOREVER :.COMMANDS
RUN :.COMMANDS
FOREVER :.COMMANDS
END

TO .REMOVE_BOOK :.NAME
IF NOT NAME? ".DISPLAYOK [MAKE ".DISPLAYOK TRUE]
IF :.DISPLAYOK [PRINT " .DISPLAY_BOOK THING :.NAME]
PRINT "
MAKE ".LP .REQUEST [PHRASE]
IF EMPTY? :.LP [STOP]
MAKE :.NAME .REM_BOOK :.LP THING :.NAME
PRINT "
.REMOVE_BOOK :.NAME
END

TO .REM_BOOK :.LP :.BOOK
IF EMPTY? :.BOOK [PRINT SE :.LP [IS NOT IN THE PHRASEBOOK] OP :.BOOK]
IF EQUAL? :.LP FIRST FIRST :.BOOK [OP BF :.BOOK]
    [OP SE FPUT FIRST :.BOOK [] .REM_BOOK :.LP BF :.BOOK]
END


TO .FINDBIT :.BOOKNAME
MAKE ".WANTED .REQUEST [PHRASE]
PRINT "
IF EMPTY? :.WANTED [STOP]
MAKE ".FOUND LOOKMATCH :.WANTED THING :.BOOKNAME
IF EMPTY? :.FOUND [PRINT SE :.WANTED [IS NOT IN THE PHRASEBOOK]]
    [IF RUNNABLE? FIRST :.FOUND [IF NOT MEMBER? FIRST :.FOUND [PRINT PR]
    [PRINT :.FOUND] [] RUN :.FOUND] [PRINT :.FOUND]]
PRINT "
.FINDBIT :.BOOKNAME
END


TO .MATCHES? :.PHRASE :.ENTRY
IF EQUAL? :.PHRASE :.ENTRY [OP TRUE]
IF EMPTY? :.ENTRY [OP FALSE]
IF AND EMPTY? :.PHRASE .?P FIRST :.ENTRY [OP FALSE]
IF EQUAL? "? FIRST FIRST :.ENTRY
    [OP .MATCHES? .CHECK :.PHRASE :.ENTRY BF :.ENTRY]
IF EMPTY? :.PHRASE [OP FALSE]
IF EQUAL? FIRST :.PHRASE FIRST :.ENTRY [OP .MATCHES? BF :.PHRASE BF :.ENTRY]
OP FALSE
END

TO .?P :.WORD
IF NOT EQUAL? FIRST :.WORD "? [OP FALSE]
MAKE ".WORD BF :.WORD
IF EMPTY? :.WORD [OP TRUE]
IF EQUAL? FIRST :.WORD "? [OP FALSE]
OP TRUE
END

TO .CHECK :.PHRASE :.ENTRY
MAKE ".WHAT FIRST :.ENTRY

IF EMPTY? BF :.WHAT [OP BF :.PHRASE]
MAKE ".WHAT BF :.WHAT
IF NOT EQUAL? FIRST :.WHAT "?
    [MAKE :.WHAT FIRST :.PHRASE MAKE ".ASSIGNED TRUE OP BF :.PHRASE]
IF EMPTY? BF :.WHAT [OP .VAR_IS_?? :.PHRASE BF :.ENTRY]
OP .MANY :.PHRASE BF :.ENTRY BF :.WHAT []
END
```

```
TO .REQUEST :.MESSAGE
TYPE :.MESSAGE
TYPE ":
.SPACES 1
OP RL
END


TO .TEACHBIT :.NAME :.DISPLAYOK
IF :.DISPLAYOK [PRINT " .DISPLAY_BOOK THING :.NAME]
PRINT "
MAKE ".LP .REQUEST [LEFT PAGE]
IF EMPTY? :.LP [PRINT " STOP]
MAKE ".RP .REQUEST [RIGHT PAGE]
IF EMPTY? :.RP [PRINT " STOP]
MAKE :.NAME INSERT :.LP :.RP THING :.NAME
.TEACHBIT :.NAME :.DISPLAYOK
END


TO .SPACES :.NUM
REPEAT :.NUM [TYPE "\ ]
END


TO .DISPLAY_ENTRY :.LP :.LSIZE :.RP :.RSIZE
IF OR ( :.LSIZE > 35 ) ( :.RSIZE > 35 ) [PRINT :.LP PRINT :.RP STOP]
IF :.RSIZE + :.LSIZE > 35 [PRINT :.LP .SPACES 37 - :.RSIZE PRINT :.RP STOP]
IF :.RSIZE > 17 [TYPE :.LP .SPACES 37 - :.RSIZE - :.LSIZE PRINT :.RP STOP]
IF :.LSIZE > 17 [TYPE :.LP .SPACES 2 PRINT :.RP]
   [TYPE :.LP .SPACES 19 - :.LSIZE PRINT :.RP]
END


TO .COUNTCHARS :.EL
IF EMPTY? :.EL [OP -1]
IF WORD? :.EL [OP COUNT :.EL]
OP 1 + ( COUNT FIRST :.EL ) + ( .COUNTCHARS BF :.EL )
END


TO .DISPLAY_BOOK :.BOOK
IF EMPTY? :.BOOK [STOP]
.DISPLAY_ENTRY ( FIRST FIRST :.BOOK ) ( .COUNTCHARS FIRST FIRST :.BOOK )
   ( FIRST BF FIRST :.BOOK ) ( .COUNTCHARS FIRST BF FIRST :.BOOK )
.DISPLAY_BOOK BF :.BOOK
END


TO .ASK_FOR_NAME :.PROMPT
MAKE ".NAME .REQUEST :.PROMPT
IF ( COUNT :.NAME ) > 1 [PRINT [OOPS - A NAME MUST BE ONE WORD]
   OP .ASK_FOR_NAME :.PROMPT]
IF EMPTY? :.NAME [OP []] [OP FIRST :.NAME]
END


TO .FILL :.RESPONSE
IF EMPTY? :.RESPONSE [OP []]
IF WORD? :.RESPONSE [OP :.RESPONSE]
IF LIST? FIRST :.RESPONSE [OP FPUT .FILL FIRST :.RESPONSE .FILL BF :.RESPONSE]
IF MEMBER? FIRST FIRST :.RESPONSE [" :]
   [OP .WORDORVAR FIRST :.RESPONSE BF :.RESPONSE]
IF OR EMPTY? BF FIRST :.RESPONSE NOT EQUAL? FIRST FIRST :.RESPONSE "?
   [OP FPUT FIRST :.RESPONSE .FILL BF :.RESPONSE]
MAKE ".WHAT BF FIRST :.RESPONSE
IF AND EQUAL? FIRST :.WHAT "? NOT EMPTY? BF :.WHAT [MAKE ".WHAT BF :.WHAT]
OP SE THING :.WHAT .FILL BF :.RESPONSE
END


TO .WORDORVAR :.FBIT :.BFBIT
IF EQUAL? COUNT :.FBIT 1 [OP SE :.FBIT :.BFBIT]
IF NOT EQUAL? FIRST BF :.FBIT "? [OP SE :.FBIT :.BFBIT]
OP SE WORD FIRST :.FBIT FIRST .FILL FPUT BF :.FBIT [] .FILL :.BFBIT
END


TO .MANY :.PHRASE :.NEXTMATCH :.VARIABLE :.MATCHBIT
IF EMPTY? :.NEXTMATCH [MAKE :.VARIABLE :.PHRASE MAKE ".ASSIGNED TRUE OP []]
IF EMPTY? :.PHRASE [OP :.PHRASE]
IF EQUAL? FIRST :.PHRASE FIRST :.NEXTMATCH
   [MAKE :.VARIABLE :.MATCHBIT MAKE ".ASSIGNED TRUE OP :.PHRASE]
OP .MANY BF :.PHRASE :.NEXTMATCH :.VARIABLE LPUT FIRST :.PHRASE :.MATCHBIT
END
```

```
TO .VAR_IS_?? :.PHRASE :.NEXTMATCH
IF OR EMPTY? :.PHRASE EMPTY? :.NEXTMATCH [OP []]
IF EQUAL? FIRST :.PHRASE FIRST :.NEXTMATCH [OP :.PHRASE]
OP .VAR_IS_?? BF :.PHRASE :.NEXTMATCH
END
```

Contents of the file FRENCH

```
MAKE "FRENCH [[[BIG] [GRAND]] [[BOOK] [LE LIVRE]] [[COME] [VENIR]] [[DOG]
    [LE CHIEN]] [[GO] [ALLER]] [[HOUSE] [LA MAISON]] [[PEN] [LE STYLO]]
    [[SMALL] [PETIT]] [[TREE] [L'ARBRE]]]
```

Contents of the file GEOG

```
MAKE "GEOGRAPHY [[[?? RIVER ?? GLASGOW ??] [CLYDE]] [[?? RIVER ?? DURHAM ??]
    [WEIR]] [[?? RIVER ?? MANCHESTER ??] [MERSEY]] [[?? RIVER ?? NOTTINGHAM ??]
    [TRENT]] [[?? RIVER ?? HEREFORD ??] [WYE]] [[?? RIVER ?? BRISTOL ??] [AVON]]
    [[?? RIVER ?? OXFORD ??] [THAMES]] [[?? RIVER ?? PLYMOUTH ??] [TAMAR]]]
```

Contents of the file RANDY

```
MAKE "RANDY [[[?? FORWARD ??] [FD RANDOM 100]] [[?? BACK ??] [BK RANDOM 50]]
    [[?? TURN ??] [RT RANDOM 360]] [[?? LEFT ??] [LT RANDOM 180]] [[?? RIGHT
    ??] [RT RANDOM 180]]]
```

Contents of the file AREA

```
MAKE "AREA [[[?? AREA OF A RECTANGLE ?X BY ?Y ??] [PRINT ?X * ?Y]]
    [[?? AREA OF A TRIANGLE ?? BASE ?X AND HEIGHT ?Y] [PRINT .5 * ?X * ?Y]]
    [[?? AREA OF A CIRCLE ?? RADIUS ?X ??] [PRINT ?X * ?X * 22 / 7]] [[?? AREA
    OF A SQUARE ?? SIDE ?X] [PRINT ?X * ?X]]]
```

Contents of the file ELIZA

```
MAKE "ELIZA [[[?? YOU ARE ??X] [WHY DO YOU THINK I AM ??X]] [[?? I ?X YOU]
    [WHY DO YOU ?X ME]] [[?? I THINK ??] [WHY DO YOU THINK THAT]]
    [[?? MOTHER ??] [TELL ME MORE ABOUT YOUR FAMILY]] [[?? DO YOU ??X ME]
    [WOULD YOU LIKE ME TO ??X YOU]]]
```

Contents of the file BOXES

```
TO PUT
PRINT "
MAKE ".BOXNAME .ASK_FOR_NAME [BOX NAME]
IF EMPTY? :.BOXNAME [PRINT " STOP]
IF NOT NAME? "BOXES [MAKE "BOXES []]
IF NOT MEMBER? FPUT :.BOXNAME [] :BOXES [MAKE :.BOXNAME [] MAKE "BOXES
    LPUT FPUT :.BOXNAME [] :BOXES]
IF NOT NAME? ".DISPLAYOK [MAKE ".DISPLAYOK TRUE]
.PUTBIT :.BOXNAME
END


TO DO
IF NOT NAME? "BOXES [MAKE "BOXES []]
PRINT "
MAKE ".PATTERN .REQUEST [WORD PATTERN]
IF EMPTY? :.PATTERN [PRINT " STOP]
PRINT "
.OUTPUT SCAN :.PATTERN
DO
END


TO LOTS
IF NOT NAME? "BOXES [MAKE "BOXES []]
PRINT "
MAKE ".PATTERN .REQUEST [WORD PATTERN]
IF EMPTY? :.PATTERN [PRINT " STOP]
PRINT "
FOREVER [IF KEY? [STOP] [.OUTPUT SCAN :.PATTERN]]
END
```

```
TO CONTENTS
MAKE ".DISPLAYOK TRUE
END

TO NOCONTENTS
MAKE ".DISPLAYOK FALSE
END

TO DISPLAY
PRINT "
MAKE ".NAME .ASK_FOR_NAME [NAME]
PRINT "
IF EMPTY? :.NAME [STOP]
IF NOT NAME? :.NAME [PRINT [OOPS - THERE IS NO BOX OR BOOK NAMED]
    PRINT :.NAME PRINT " STOP]
IF WORD? FIRST THING :.NAME [PRINT THING :.NAME PRINT " STOP]
IF WORD? FIRST FIRST THING :.NAME [.DISPLAY_BOX THING :.NAME]
    [.DISPLAY_BOOK THING :.NAME]
PRINT "
END

TO INBOX :.ITEM :.BOX
IF NOT MEMBER? :.ITEM :.BOX [OP LPUT :.ITEM :.BOX] [OP :.BOX]
END

TO SCAN :.PATTERN
IF EMPTY? :.PATTERN [OP []]
IF LIST? FIRST :.PATTERN [OP SE FPUT SCAN FIRST :.PATTERN [] SCAN BF :.PATTERN]
OP SE .LOOKAT FIRST :.PATTERN SCAN BF :.PATTERN
END

TO FOREVER :.IL
RUN :.IL
FOREVER :.IL
END

TO RUNNABLE? :WORD
OP MEMBER? :WORD [PR PRINT SHOW TYPE RUN REPEAT TOPLEVEL CLEAN CT CS HOME
    HT PD PU ST FD FORWARD BK BACK LEFT LT RIGHT RT SETBG SETC SETH SETPC SETPOS
    SETX SETY]
END

TO .PPRINT :.LIST
IF EMPTY? :.LIST [PRINT [] STOP]
IF EQUAL? FIRST :.LIST "& [PRINT []] [TYPE FIRST :.LIST TYPE "\ ]
.PPRINT BF :.LIST
END

TO REMOVE
PRINT "
MAKE ".NAME .ASK_FOR_NAME [NAME]
PRINT "
IF EMPTY? :.NAME [STOP]
IF NOT NAME? :.NAME [PRINT [OOPS - THERE IS NO BOX OR BOOK NAMED]
    PRINT :.NAME PRINT " STOP]
IF WORD? FIRST FIRST THING :.NAME [.REMOVE_BOX :.NAME] [.REMOVE_BOOK :.NAME]
PRINT "
END

TO .REMOVE_BOX :.NAME
IF :.DISPLAYOK [.DISPLAY_BOX THING :.NAME]
PRINT "
MAKE ".ITEM .REQUEST [ITEM]
PRINT "
IF EMPTY? :.ITEM [STOP]
IF ( AND EQUAL? :.NAME "BOXES EQUAL? COUNT :.ITEM 1 MEMBER? :.ITEM :BOXES )
    [ER FPUT WORD "" FIRST :.ITEM []]
MAKE :.NAME .REM_BOX :.ITEM THING :.NAME
IF AND EMPTY? THING :.NAME NOT ( :.NAME = "BOXES ) [MAKE "BOXES .REM_BOX
    FPUT :.NAME [] :BOXES ER FPUT WORD "" :.NAME [] STOP]
.REMOVE_BOX :.NAME
END

TO .REM_BOX :.ITEM :.BOX
IF EMPTY? :.BOX [PRINT SE :.ITEM [IS NOT IN THE BOX] OP :.BOX]
IF NOT EQUAL? :.ITEM FIRST :.BOX [OP FPUT FIRST :.BOX .REM_BOX :.ITEM
    BF :.BOX STOP]
OP BF :.BOX
END
```

```
TO .ADDTOVOCAB :.BOXNAME :.RESPONSE
IF NOT MEMBER? FPUT :.BOXNAME [] :BOXES [MAKE :.BOXNAME [] MAKE "BOXES LPUT
    FPUT :.BOXNAME [] :BOXES]
IF NOT MEMBER? :.RESPONSE THING :.BOXNAME [MAKE :.BOXNAME LPUT :.RESPONSE
    THING :.BOXNAME]
END

TO .CHOOSE :.PART
IF NOT MEMBER? FPUT :.PART [] :BOXES [OP FPUT :.PART []]
OP ITEM ( RANDOM COUNT THING :.PART ) + 1 THING :.PART
END

TO .INPUT :.PATBIT
MAKE ".PATBIT FPUT :.PATBIT []
MAKE ".INWORD .REQUEST :.PATBIT

IF EMPTY? :.INWORD [OP :.PATBIT]
IF NOT EQUAL? :.PATBIT :.INWORD [.ADDTOVOCAB FIRST :.PATBIT :.INWORD]
OP :.INWORD
END

TO .LOOKAT :.PATBIT
IF EQUAL? FIRST :.PATBIT "# [MAKE ".CHOICE .INPUT BF :.PATBIT]
   [MAKE ".CHOICE .CHOOSE :.PATBIT]
IF EQUAL? FIRST :.CHOICE :.PATBIT [OP FIRST :.CHOICE] [OP SCAN :.CHOICE]
END

TO .ASK_FOR_NAME :.PROMPT
MAKE ".NAME .REQUEST :.PROMPT
IF ( COUNT :.NAME ) > 1 [PRINT [OOPS - A NAME MUST BE ONE WORD]
   OP .ASK_FOR_NAME :PROMPT]
IF EMPTY? :.NAME [OP []] [OP FIRST :.NAME]
END

TO .DISPLAY_BOX :.BOX
IF EMPTY? :.BOX [STOP]
PRINT FIRST :.BOX
.DISPLAY_BOX BF :.BOX
END

TO .PUTBIT :.BOXNAME
IF :.DISPLAYOK [PRINT " .DISPLAY_BOX THING :.BOXNAME]
PRINT "
MAKE ".ITEM .REQUEST [ITEM]
IF EMPTY? :.ITEM [PRINT " STOP]
MAKE :.BOXNAME INBOX :.ITEM THING :.BOXNAME
.PUTBIT :.BOXNAME
END

TO .SPACES :.NUM
REPEAT :.NUM [TYPE "\ ]
END

TO .OUTPUT :.OUTLIST
IF RUNNABLE? FIRST :.OUTLIST [RUN :.OUTLIST] [.PPRINT :.OUTLIST]
END

TO .REQUEST :.MESSAGE
TYPE :.MESSAGE
TYPE ":
.SPACES 1
OP RL
END
```

Contents of the file FARM

```
MAKE "BOXES [[SENTENCE] [NOUNPHRASE] [NOUN] [VERB] [ADJECTIVE]]
MAKE ".ITEM []
MAKE ".PATTERN []
MAKE ".BOXNAME "ADJECTIVE
MAKE ".DISPLAYOK "TRUE
MAKE ".CHOICE [DONKEY ]
MAKE ".NAME [ADJECTIVE]
MAKE "SENTENCE [[NOUNPHRASE VERB NOUNPHRASE]]
MAKE "VERB [[EATS] [TICKLES] [DEVOURS]]
MAKE "ADJECTIVE [[SPOTTED] [SILLY] [HAIRY]]
MAKE "NOUN [[WOMBAT] [DONKEY] [DOG]]
MAKE "NOUNPHRASE [[THE NOUN] [THE ADJECTIVE NOUN]]
```

Contents of the file HAIKU

```
MAKE "BOXES [[SENTENCE] [NP] [VP] [VERB] [ADJECTIVE] [NOUN] [HAIKU] [LINE1]
    [LINE] [LINE2] [LINE3] [VERBT]]
MAKE "SENTENCE [[NP VP]]
MAKE "VERB [[TUMBLES] [FLOWS] [FALLS] [RISES] [HOVERS] [OPENS] [SHIMMERS]]
MAKE "NOUN [[CLOUD] [RIVER] [STREAM] [MOUNTAIN] [LEAF] [BUD] [EAGLE] [SWALLOW]]
MAKE "ADJECTIVE [[SLOW] [BRIGHT] [FRAGRANT] [SHIMMERING] [SOFT] [WARM] [TIMID]]
MAKE "HAIKU [[LINE1 & LINE2 & LINE3 & &]]
MAKE "NP [[THE NOUN] [THE ADJECTIVE NOUN]]
MAKE "VP [[VERB NP]]
MAKE "VERBT [[GREETS] [WELCOMES] [MEETS] [STARTLES]]
MAKE "LINE3 [[VERBT THE ADJECTIVE NOUN]]
MAKE "LINE2 [[ADJECTIVE NOUN VERB AND]]
MAKE "LINE1 [[ADJECTIVE ADJECTIVE NOUN VERB]]
```

Contents of the file ADVENT

```
TO ADVENTURE
IF DEFINED? "LOTS [ER [LOTS DO SCAN .LOOKAT CONTENTS NOCONTENTS]]
EXPLORE FIRST :PLACES
END


TO CREATE
PRINT "
MAKE "PLACE .ASK_FOR_NAME [PLACE NAME]
PR []
IF EMPTY? :PLACE [STOP]
IF NOT NAME? "PLACES [MAKE "PLACES []]
IF NOT MEMBER? :PLACE :PLACES [MAKE :PLACE [] MAKE WORD :PLACE ".O []]
    [LOAD :PLACE]
IF NOT NAME? ".DISPLAYOK [MAKE ".DISPLAYOK TRUE]
TS
PR [CREATE A PROCEDURE THAT WILL BE]
TYPE [RUN WHEN YOU ENTER] .SPACES 1
PR :PLACE
PR [END WITH < CTRL C >]
WAIT 220
EDIT :PLACE
PR [ADD THE COMMANDS TO MOVE FROM]
PR :PLACE
.TEACHBIT :PLACE TRUE
PR []
PR [NOW ADD THE ITEMS TO BE FOUND AT]
PR :PLACE
.PUTBIT WORD :PLACE ".O
IF MEMBER? :PLACE :PLACES [*DELETE :PLACE] [MAKE "PLACES LPUT :PLACE :PLACES]
TIDY :PLACE
END


TO STORE :PLACE
*DELETE :PLACE
SAVE :PLACE ( SE WORD "" :PLACE :PLACE ( WORD "" :PLACE ".O ) )
ER ( SE WORD "" :PLACE :PLACE ( WORD "" :PLACE ".O ) )
END


TO READIN :PLACE
LOAD :PLACE
TS
RUN FPUT :PLACE []
MAKE "OBJECTS THING WORD :PLACE ".O
IF NOT EMPTY? :OBJECTS [PR [YOU CAN SEE:] PR [] .DISPLAY_BOX :OBJECTS]
END


TO EXPLORE :PLACE
IF NOT DEFINED? :PLACE [READIN :PLACE]
MAKE "NEW EXPLOREBIT :PLACE
IF EQUAL? :NEW "KILLED [PR [OOPS - YOU HAVE GOT YOURSELF KILLED] STOP]
IF EQUAL? :NEW "FINISHED [PR " PR [GAME FINISHED. TO RESTART IT,]
    PR SE [TYPE: EXPLORE] WORD "" :PLACE STOP]
IF EQUAL? :NEW :PLACE [EXPLORE :PLACE] [STORE :PLACE EXPLORE :NEW]
END
```

```
TO EXPLOREBIT :PLACE
PRINT []
TYPE [WHAT DO YOU WANT TO DO?]
MAKE "COMMAND RL
IF :COMMAND = [] [( *DELETE :PLACE ) TIDY :PLACE OP "FINISHED]
MAKE "NEW LOOKMATCH :COMMAND THING :PLACE
IF EQUAL? COUNT :NEW 1 [OP FIRST :NEW]
IF EMPTY? :NEW [TRY_OWN :COMMAND MAKE WORD :PLACE ".O :OBJECTS OP :PLACE]
IF NOT EQUAL? FIRST :NEW "IF [PR :NEW OP :PLACE]
MAKE "NEW RUN :NEW
RUN BF :NEW
OP FIRST :NEW
END

TO TRY_OWN :COMMAND
MAKE "NEW LOOKMATCH :COMMAND :OWN
IF EMPTY? :NEW [PR [I DON'T UNDERSTAND THAT COMMAND] STOP]
RUN :NEW
END

TO HOLDING? :OBJECTS
IF :OBJECTS = [] [OP TRUE]
IF NOT MEMBER? FIRST :OBJECTS :OWN.O [OP FALSE]
OP HOLDING? BF :OBJECTS :OWN.O
END

TO ADD :ITEM
PR [YOU ARE NOW HOLDING A]
PR :ITEM
MAKE "OWN.O INBOX :ITEM :OWN.O
END

TO PICKUP :X
IF NOT MEMBER? :X :OBJECTS [PR [] PR ( SE [I SEE NO] :X [HERE] ) PR [] STOP]
PR []
MAKE "OBJECTS .REM_BOX :X :OBJECTS
MAKE "OWN.O INBOX :X :OWN.O
PR [OK]
PR []
END

TO SCRAP :ITEM
MAKE "OWN.O .REM_BOX :ITEM :OWN.O
END

TO PUTDOWN :X
IF NOT MEMBER? :X :OWN.O [PR [] PR [YOU ARE NOT HOLDING THAT] PR [] STOP]
PR []
MAKE "OWN.O .REM_BOX :X :OWN.O
MAKE "OBJECTS INBOX :X :OBJECTS
PR [OK]
PR []
END

TO TIDY :PLACE
SAVE :PLACE ( SE :PLACE WORD "" :PLACE ( WORD "" :PLACE ".O ) )
ER ( SE :PLACE WORD "" :PLACE ( WORD "" :PLACE ".O ) )
*DELETE ADVENT
SAVE "ADVENT [STORE READIN ADVENTURE EXPLORE EXPLOREBIT TRY_OWN HOLDING?
    ADD CREATE PICKUP SCRAP PUTDOWN TIDY "PLACES "OWN "OWN.O]
END

MAKE "PLACES [BEACH HILL FOREST FOREST1 FOREST2 CAVE HALL]
MAKE "OWN [[[TAKE THE ??X] [PICKUP [??X]]] [[PICK UP THE ??X]
    [PICKUP [??X]]] [[DROP THE ??X] [PUTDOWN [??X]]] [[LIGHT ?? TWIGS] [IF
    HOLDING? [[BOX OF MATCHES] [SMALL TWIGS]] [SCRAP [SMALL TWIGS] ADD [FLAMING
    TORCH]] [PR [YOU DON'T HAVE THE MEANS]]]] [[INVENTORY] [.DISPLAY_BOX
    :OWN.O]] [[WHAT ?? CARRYING] [.DISPLAY_BOX :OWN.O]]]
MAKE "OWN.O []
```

Contents of the file BEACH

```
TO BEACH
PR [YOU ARE STANDING ON A BEACH]
PR [TO THE SOUTH OF A STEEP HILL.]
PR [A PATH LEADS WEST.]
END
```

```
MAKE "BEACH [[[?? CLIMB ?? HILL ??] [HILL]] [[?? NORTH ??] [HILL]]
    [[?? WEST ??] [FOREST]] [[?? SOUTH ??] [KILLED]] [[?? EAST ??] [YOU ARE
    STOPPED BY A SHEER CLIFF]] [[GO UP ??] [HILL]]]
```

```
MAKE "BEACH.O [[BOX OF MATCHES]]
```

Contents of the file FOREST

```
TO FOREST
PR [YOU ARE IN A FOREST AT THE FOOT]
PR [OF A STEEP HILL.]
PR [PATHS LEAD OFF IN ALL DIRECTIONS.]
END
```

```
MAKE "FOREST [[[?? EAST ??] [BEACH]] [[?? WEST ??] [FOREST1]] [[?? NORTH ??]
    [THE TREES ARE TOO THICK]] [[?? SOUTH ??] [THE TREES ARE TOO THICK]]
    [[CLIMB ?? HILL ??] [HILL]] [[GO UP] [HILL]]]
```

```
MAKE "FOREST.O [[SMALL TWIGS]]
```

Contents of the file FOREST1

```
TO FOREST1
PR [YOU ARE IN A DEEP DARK FOREST]
END
```

```
MAKE "FOREST1 [[[?? NORTH ??] [FOREST]] [[?? WEST ??] [FOREST2]]
    [[?? EAST ??] [FOREST2]] [[?? SOUTH ??] [FOREST2]] [[?? CLIMB ?? TREE ??]
    [THE BRANCHES ARE TOO HIGH TO REACH]]]
```

```
MAKE "FOREST1.O []
```

Contents of the file FOREST2

```
TO FOREST2
PR [YOU ARE IN A DEEP DARK FOREST]
END
```

```
MAKE "FOREST2 [[[?? WEST ??] [FOREST1]] [[?? EAST ??] [FOREST2]]
    [[?? SOUTH ??] [FOREST2]] [[?? NORTH ??] [FOREST2]] [[?? CLIMB ?? TREE ??]
    [THE BRANCHES ARE TOO HIGH TO REACH]]]
```

```
MAKE "FOREST2.O []
```

Contents of the file HILL

```
TO HILL
PR [YOU ARE STANDING ON THE SIDE OF A STEEP]
PR [HILL ABOVE A SANDY BEACH.]

PR [A SMALL HOLE LEADS INTO THE HILLSIDE.]
END
```

```
MAKE "HILL [[[?? WALK DOWN ??] [BEACH]] [[?? ENTER ?? HOLE ??] [CAVE]]
    [[GO IN ??] [CAVE]] [[?? DOWN ?? HOLE] [CAVE]] [[?? DOWN ?? HILL] [BEACH]]
    [[GO DOWN] [BEACH]]]
```

```
MAKE "HILL.O []
```

Contents of the file CAVE

```
TO CAVE
PR [YOU ARE IN A CAVE CARVED IN THE]
PR [HILLSIDE. A LIGHT SHINES DIMLY THROUGH]
PR [A SMALL HOLE FAR ABOVE YOU.]
PR [ELVISH RUNES ARE SCRATCHED ON THE]
PR [CAVE WALLS.]
IF HOLDING? [[FLAMING TORCH]] [PR [A PASSAGE LEADS DOWNWARDS.]]
    [PR [IT IS DARK IN HERE. IF YOU GO ON] PR [YOU MAY FALL DOWN A PIT.]]
END
```

```
MAKE "CAVE [[[CLIMB ?? HOLE ??] [IT IS TOO HIGH TO REACH]] [[?? UP ??]
    [THE HOLE IS TOO HIGH TO REACH]] [[?? DOWN ??] [IF HOLDING? [[FLAMING
    TORCH]] [[HALL]] [[KILLED PR [YOU FELL DOWN A PIT]]]]] [[WAVE ?? ROD ??]
    [IF HOLDING? [[RUSTY ROD]] [[HILL]] [[CAVE]]]] [[READ THE RUNES] [IF TRUE
    [[CAVE TYPE CHAR 147 REPEAT 20 [TYPE CHAR ( 161 + RANDOM 30 )] PR []]]]]]

MAKE "CAVE.O [[RUSTY ROD]]
```

Contents of the file HALL

```
TO HALL
PR [YOU ARE IN A VAST HALL WITH]
PR [A HIGH VAULTED CEILING CARVED]
PR [OUT OF STONE.]
PR [A SMALL PASSAGE LEADS UP AND NORTH.]
END

MAKE "HALL [[[?? UP ??] [CAVE]] [[?? NORTH ??] [CAVE]]]

MAKE "HALL.O [[ELVISH GOLD]]
```

Appendix 2

Diagnostic test of language manipulation skills, with specimen answers

1. THE PASSAGE BELOW READS VERY STRANGELY. CAN YOU RE-WRITE IT SO AS TO IMPROVE THE GRAMMAR? FOR EXAMPLE 'years of work hard' SHOULD BE CHANGED TO 'years of hard work'.

   After years of work hard the mad professor has finished his robot which were five feet tall with strong arms. The professor could made its robot move, though it was a slowly walker. If there are any intruders at the night the robot was programmed to attack him.

   After years of hard work the mad professor had finished his robot, which was five feet tall, with strong arms. The professor could make his robot move, though it was a slow walker. If there were any intruders at night, the robot was programmed to attack them.

2. ALL THE SENTENCES BELOW CONTAIN MISTAKES OF GRAMMAR FOR EACH SENTENCE IN THE LEFT COLUMN, FIND ONE IN THE RIGHT COLUMN WITH A SIMILAR MISTAKE. FOR EXAMPLE, a) PAIRS WITH 5).

THEN EXPLAIN, AS CLEARLY AS POSSIBLE, WHAT IS WRONG
WITH EACH PAIR.

a) She eated the cream cake
b) Girl is at the door.

c) I am knowing your sister.

d) The quickly boy ran to the tree.
e) The colour green hates George.
f) I see the lion and felt frightrned.

1) I am liking the ice cream.
2) The happily girl plays on the swing.
3) He drove the car into the wall and smash it.
4) Golf plays my sister.
5) I knowed the boy.
6) Cat sits on the rug.

a) pairs with 5)

Mistake: Normally. you. form the past tense of a verb by adding 'ed' to the present tense, but 'know' and 'eat' are different. Their past tenses should be 'knew' and 'ate'.

b) pairs with 6.

Mistake: The article ('a' or 'the') is missing before the first noun in each sentence.

c) pairs with 1.

Mistake: 'Know' and 'like' are two verbs which cannot form the present participle. ('I am knowing' should be 'I know).

d) Pairs with 2.

Mistake: The adverb is in the wrong place in the sentences (it should be after the verb, or at the start of the sentence).

e) pairs with 4.

Mistake: The nouns in each sentence are in the

. . . .

wrong order, so the sentences are meaningless.

f) pairs with 3.

Mistake: The tenses of the verbs are mixed.
The sentences should either be in the past
or the present tense.

3. CHANGE EACH WORD IN THE SENTENCES BELOW INTO A SIMILAR
    WORD (WITH THE SAME PART OF SPEECH). THE NEW SENTENCE
    WILL HAVE THE SAME PATTERN AS THE OLD ONE, BUT A DIFFER-
    ENT MEANING (THE FIRST HAS BEEN DONE FOR YOU).

a) The   cat   sits   on   the   mat.
    A   boy   runs   down a   street.

b) She   ate   the   cake   with   a   fork.
    He   kicked a   ball   over   the wall

c) At   the   top   of   the   tree
    In   a   house by   the   river

    sits   a   little   bird.
    lives   an   old   man

d) Who   runs   fastest?
    Which sounds loudest?

(e) Kick   the   ball.
     Throw   the   spear

4. THE SENTENCES BELOW ARE IN PAIRS. THE FIRST ONE OF EACH
    PAIR HAS BEEN CHANGED INTO A NEW SENTENCE WITH THE
    SAME MEANING. CHANGE THE SECOND SENTENCE OF THE PAIR
    IN THE SAME WAY.

OLD SENTENCE	CHANGED SENTENCE

a)   Mary ate the ice cream → The ice cream was eaten by Mary.

The lion bit the explorer → **The explorer was bitten by the lion.**

b)   The headmaster gave a prize to Jane. → Jane was given a prize by the headmaster.

The postman handed a letter to John. → **John was handed a letter by the postman.**

c)   A man was sitting on the bench. → There was a man sitting on the bench.

Fairies are living at the bottom of my garden. → **There are fairies living at the bottom of my garden.**

5.   REWRITE EACH OF THE GROUPS OF SENTENCES AS ONE SENTENCE. THE NEW SENTENCE SHOULD BE GOOD ENGLISH AND EASY TO READ. THE FIRST HAS BEEN DONE FOR YOU.

a)   The boy has a red bicycle. He lives next door.
The boy who lives next door has a red bicycle.

b)   The girl jumps down from the tree. The tree is tall.

The girl jumps down from the tall tree.

c)   The princess eats the cake. It was baked by the evil witch.

The princess eats the cake, which was baked by the evil witch.

d) Mary walked up to the house. The house was old. Mary knocked on the door.

Mary walked up to the old house and knocked on the door.

e) The girl walks down the street. The girl is good looking. She is young. She is carrying a purse. The purse is red.

The young good looking girl walks down the street carrying a red purse.

6. CHANGE THESE SENTENCES INTO MORE INTERESTING DESCRIPTIONS. THE FIRST HAS BEEN DONE FOR YOU.

a) The cat sat on the rug.
The lazy tabby cat sat, as still as a china statue, on the rug beside the fire.

b) The boy ate an ice cream.

c) The car slid across the road.

. . . .

. . . .

d)   The rocket took off.

. . . .

. . . .

. . . .

. . . .

Appendix 3

First and final versions of the 'Haunted House' stories

James

On a stormy night in 1907 two campers were running down a windey country
road. Suddenly in front of their eyes a poor old man appeared. He said to them
in a stubborn, croaky voice, "If your'r lookin for shelter, there's an old mansion (ancient castle)
down the road, turn left and your there, but be careful it's ! itssss". "Somehow
he's gone, that's funny". The campers did what the old man had told them, and *elderly*
they found the ~~old~~ mansion. The gates were solid iron, luckily they were open
enough that the campers could slip through. They both started walking up to
the mansion doors and they saw a sign which said RING BELL BEFORE
ENTERING OR DEATH. The rest of the writing had faded away. The campers
rang the door bell and ~~old~~ man opened the doors and said, "What do you want". (he was wearing a dinner jacket and tails)
an
They answered, "We only want some food and a roof over us for the night. The
their
old butler agreed and showed them up to there room. The door was oak and it
had a metal door handle. They both entered there room and found two 4
posted bedrooms, with bedclothes all ready for them. Somehow the butler had
walked in the room and said "Dinner is ready. The campers asked if they could

have it in there room. Two minutes later the butler arrived at the door with
two trays on a trolley. They had both got tucked into ~~there~~ *their* dinner when suddenly one of the campers pulled out a 3 inch nail from his chicken. There was some
blood on the end. He put the nail in his rucksack and then he went to his bed.
The two campers had gone to bed and fallen asleep but they were lucky to be
under there covers because the butler walked into ~~there room with a bread knife~~ *their*
and slipped out again. They had leaned on a button and fallen down a trap door.
In the middle of the night they both found themselves at the bottom of a pit.
Then suddenly a bunch of monsters started approaching them slowly. There was a
jolly wobbles
slithery blobs
slimy bubbles
werewolfs
Draculas
Mummy's
and slimes.
They all gobbled up the campers and went back to there dungeons.

James
THE (FAMOUS) NIGHTMARE MYSTERY.

On a stormy night in 1907 two campers were running down a windey country road. Suddenly in front of their eyes a poor old man appeard. He said to them in a stubborn, croaky voice, "If your'r lookin for shelter, there's an ancient castle down the road, turn left and your there, but be careful it's ! itsss". "Somehow he's gone, that's funny". The campers did what the elderly man had told them, and they found the mansion. The gates were solid iron, luckily they were open enough that the campers could slip through. They both started walking up to the mansion doors and they saw a sign which said RING THE BELL BEFORE ENTERING OR DEATH. The rest of the writing had faded away. The campers rang the door bell and man opened the doors (he was wearing a dinner jacket and tails) and said, "What do you want". They answered, "We only want some food and a roof over us for the night. The old butler agreed and showed them up to their room. The door was oak and it had a metal door handle. They both entered their room and found two 4 posted bedrooms, with bedclothes all ready for them. Somehow the butler had walked in the room and said "Dinner is ready. The campers asked if they could have it in their room. Two minutes later the butler arrived at the door with two trays on a trolley. They had both got tucked into their dinner when suddenly one of the campers pulled out a 3 inch nail from his chicken. There was some blood on the end. He put the nail in his rucksack and then he went to his bed. The two campers had gone to bed and fallen asleep but they were lucky to be under their covers because the butler walked into their room with a bread knife and slipped out again.

In the morning they both got up and yawned. Then they started to dress. Suddenly one of the campers found blood at the corner of the bedroom wall. The wall had plain whitish wall-paper, but it was a bit grotty with cobwebs and dust. Then after the campers had got dressed they heard the breakfast bell ringing. Then they both hurried quickly down the stairs and into the dining room. Beside the dark brown oak table before them stood a kitchen maid. She said to them in a squeaky voice, "If you'd both like please breakfasts are coming". They could smell some bacon and they could hear it sizzling away. After they had eaten, both of them went for some fresh air. One camper made towards the big oak tree forests. He shouted to his friend to hurry up and come with him for a walk through the forest. He never got an answer, so he started towards the bushland. Suddenly he heard some scuffling behind a gorse bush. He thought he saw a man running away. The camper felt dizzy, then he fainted. When he woke up he found himself surrounded by werewolfs. He muttered a word, and the beasts killed him. They were shaped like a man an they were hairy. Then suddenly he woke up in his bed in his tent and there beside him was his sleeping friend. So all the werewolves, the castle and the blood were just one big dream.

Dorothy and Louise

A detective came to (a) haunted (house), ~~because~~ he was going to investigate ~~the~~
an old manor *the*
murder of a friend
~~haunted house. Because a friend's body had been found there.~~ The friend had
been murdered while staying over night, because he was a ghost hunter. ~~Who~~
He was staying there. He
came because he wanted to find the Mummy of Tutankamen. He was found
murdered beside Tutankamen's tomb. The detective walked up to the porch
wooden
of the big ~~house,~~ ~~He~~ knocked at the ~~big~~ oak door, the door opened with a
manor *large*
enormous creaking sound. An old butler appeared and asked "Whom seeketh
thou this evening?". Suddenly ! a ~~big~~ black bat flew down from the lintel
giant
above the oak door. The detective asked "May I enter?" He (walks) in . . . .
steped
As he (walks) up some of the spiral stairs . . . He hears a scream he runs into a
tread
small room he sees a corpse lying on a four poster bed. He hears fast footsteps
behind him. . . . The door opens in (walks) frankenstein. The detective runs
Stamped
through a door which leads to a dining room the table is set for four three places
are filled one with the green lady one with the butler the other with oozy slime.
The green lady asks him to join in the feast. He (walks) towards the table and sits
walked
down. The slime starts to wobble he gets up and run to window. . . It was
locked he (walks) slowly towards green lady she screams he runs towards the door
creeped
and (goes) back down the spiral stairs. He sees a door he (goes) through it leads
dissapeared *derarted*
into a dark dingy kitchen, in the kitchen there was a (cheif) he had an enormous
chief
kitchen knife in his hands. He runs towards detective, detective runs towards
small stairs which leads to cellar he looks towards Tutankamun's tomb he has a
scrole in his hand the detective picks up the scrole and begins to read the (scrole)
＊ Scvol
says

TUTENKAMUN'S CURSE

A detective came to an old haunted manor, because he was going to investigate
the murder of a friend. The friend had been murdered while staying over night.
He was staying there because he was a ghost hunter. He came because he wanted
to find the Mummy of Tutankamen. He was found murdered beside Tutankamen's tomb. The detective walked up to the wooden porch of the manor. He
knocked at the large oak door, the door opened with a enormous creaking

sound. An old butler appeared and asked" Whom seeketh thou this evening?". Suddenly ! a giant black bat flew down from the lintel above the oak door. The detective asked "May I enter?" He stepped in . . . .

As he treads up some of the spiral stairs . . . He hears a scream he runs into a small room he sees a corpse lying on a four poster bed. He hears fast footsteps behind him . . . . The door opens in stamps frankenstein, The detective runs through a door which leads to a dining room the table is set for four three places are filled one with the green lady one with the butler the other with oozy slime. The green lady asks him to join in the feast. He walks towards the table and sits down. The slime strarts to wobble he gets up and run to window . . . It is locked he creeps slowly towards green lady she screams he runs towards the door and disappears back down the spiral stairs. He sees a door he goes through it leads into a dark dingy kitchen, in the kitchen there was a chef, he had an enormous kitchen knife in his hands. He runs towards detective, detective runs towards small stairs which leads to cellar. The detective looks around the cellar he doesn't see anything suddenly in the corner of his eye he sees a sparkle he walked towards the sparkling gem he noticed that it was the handle of a scroll he picks it up an begins to read the scroll it says . . . .

Here lies TUTENKAMUN
I rise from the dead
"BEWARE !" For anyone
who takes this scrole
and reads these words
are sure to die before
midnight

Suddenly he hears a creaking from a funny shaped box . . . . . .

Next day he was found by police dead with the scroll in his hand beside Tutenkamun's tomb. Now the detective knows what happened to his friend.

Sharon

THE MYSTERY OF
THE WEIRD NOISES

I am a detective I have come to the house of mystery because on December the 25th there were strange noises coming from the house. Its probably just bats or rats but I dont think so the something funny going on the house looks dull and damp. There is a wooden door it looks as if it has not been used for years whats that noise chairs rattling oh god what is this house its getting nearer he's headless good a man he has no head. Oh god. He didn't see me good. A bedroom cobwebs everywhere click somebody locked me in there is a women at the far end there is a women she is green her teeth are red shes coming for me. Gun where's weres my gun? here bang bang bang bang she not dead but shes ran went away the bullets went through her. oh ah I've fallen fell through the door to a dark pitch theres scuffling going on a rat oh my god its they are as big as me bang its dead. I here somebody coming down the steps I better hide theres a box click this is quite nice and comfy tap on the shoulder good morning I say "good morning" pause ahh dracula. A The pit is filled with mummies, bats, skeletons, ghosts, corpses, werewolf, ahh they told me not to come hear 3 detectives have came here and never been seen again, but Im one of those people once they get a mystery they wont let it go.

try to escape everyway I look there is

Sharon

I am a detective I have come to the house of mystery because on December the 25th there were strange noises coming from the house. Its probably just bats or rats but I don't think so the something funny going on the house looks dull and damp. There is a wooden door it looks as if it has not been used for years what's that noise chairs rattling oh god what is this house its getting nearer he's headless. Oh god. He didn't see me good. A bedroom cobwebs everywhere click somebody locked me in there is a women at the far end there is a women she is green her teeth are red shes coming for me. Gun where's my gun? here. bang bang bang bang, she not dead but shes ran away, the bullets went through her. oh ah I've fallen through the door to a dark pitch there's scuffling going on a rat oh my god its as big as me, bang its dead. I here sombody coming down the steps I better hide theres a box click this is quite nice and comfy tap on the shoulder "good morning" I say "good morning" pause "ahh dracula''. try to escape everyway I look there is mummies, bats, skeletons, ghosts, corpses, werewolf, ahh they told me not to come hear 3 detectives have came here and never been seen again, but I'm one of the those people once they get a mystery they wont let it go.

References

Abelson, H., di Sessa, A. (1981) *Turtle Geometry; the Computer as a Medium for Exploring Mathematics,* MIT Press, Cambridge, Mass.

Allen, D. (1980) *English Teaching Since 1965: How Much Growth?* Heinemann Educational Books, London.

Armbruster, B. B., Anderson, T. H. (1981) 'Mapping: Representing Text Structure Diagrammatically', In *Conceptual Readability; New Ways to Look at Text,* A. Rubin (Editor) Reading Education Report No. 31, Center for the Study of Reading, University of Illinois at Urbana-Champaign, Illinois.

Austin, H. (1974) 'A Computational view of the Skill of Juggling', A.I. Memo 330 (Logo Memo No. 17), Artificial Intelligence Laboratory, Massachusetts Institute of Technology, Cambridge, Mass.

Bamberger, J. (1972) 'Developing a Musical Ear', A.I. Memo 264 (Logo Memo No. 6), Artificial Intelligence Laboratory, Massachusetts Institute of Technology, Cambridge, Mass.

Bates, M., Wilson, K. (1981) 'Iliad': Interactive Language Instruction Assistance for the Deaf', Report No. 4771. Bolt, Beranek, and Newman Inc., Boston, Mass.

Bereiter, C., Scardamalia, M. (1982) 'From Conversation to Composition: the Role of Instruction in a Developmental Process' in *Advances in Instructional Psychology,* Volume 2, R. Glaser (Editor), Lawrence Erlbaum Associates, Hillsdale, N.J.

Boden, M. A. (1979) *Piaget,* Fontana/Collins, Glasgow.

Bohanon, J. N. (1976) 'Normal and Scrambled Grammar in Discrimination and Comprehension', *Child Development,* **47,** 669—681.

Borning, A. H. (1979) 'Thinglab — A Constraint-oriented Simulation Laboratory', Ph.D. Dissertation, Department of Computer Science, Stanford University.

Britton, J., Burgess, T., Martin, N., Mcleod, A., Rosen, H. (1975) *The Development of Writing Abilities (11—18),* Schools Council, London.

Britton, J., Martin, N. C., Rosen, H. (1966) 'Abilities to Write'. *New Education*, **2**, 10.

Brown, P. (1975) 'Review of "Language in Use" '. *Teaching English*, **8**, 3, 65.

Burstall, R. M., Collins, J. S., Popplestone, R. (1971) *Programming in POP-2*, Edinburgh University Press, Edinburgh.

Carbonell, J. R. (1970) 'Mixed-initiative Man-computer Instructional Dialogs', Report No. 1971, Bolt, Berenek, and Newman Inc., Cambridge, Mass.

Chafe, W. (1977) *The recall and verbalization of past experience*, in press, New York.

Chandler, D. (1982) 'The Potential of the Microcomputer in the English Classroom, in *New Directions in English Teaching*, A. Adams (Editor), The Falmer Press, Sussex.Chomsky, N. (1965) *Aspects of the Theory of Syntax*, M.I.T. Press, Cambridge, Mass.

Clark, M. (1983) Personal communication.

Collins, A., Bruce, B., Rubin, A. (1982) 'Microcomputer-based Writing Activities of the Upper Elementary Grades' in *Proceedings of the Fourth International Congress and Exposition of the Society for Applied Learning Technology, Orlando, Florida.*

Collins A., Gentner, D. (1981) 'A Framework for Cognitive Theory of Writing', in *Cognitive Processes in Writing: an Interdisciplinary Approach*, L. W. Gregg, E. Steinberg (Editors), Lawrence Erlbaum Associates, Hillsdale, N.J.

Cooper, C. R., Matsuhashi, A. (1983) 'A Theory of the Writing Process', in *The Psychology of Written Language*, M. Martlew (Editor), John Wiley and Sons, Chichester.

Corcoran, G. B. (1970) *Language Arts in the Elementary School*, The Ronald Press Company, New York.

Dansereau, D. (1978) 'The Development of a Learning Strategies Curriculum', in *Learning Strategies*, H. F. O'Neil, (Editor), Academic Press, New York.

Department of Education and Science (1975) *A Language for Life* (The Bullock Report), H.M.S.O., London.

Di Sessa, A. A. (1975) 'ORBIT': A Mini-environment for Exploring Orbital Mechanisms', in *Computers in Education*, Lecarme, O., Lewis, R. (Editors), North Holland, Amsterdam.

Dixon, J. (1975) *Growth Through English, Set in the Perspective of the Seventies*, (third edition), Oxford University Press, Oxford.

Donaldson, M., (1978a) *Children's Minds*, Fontana/Collins, Glasgow.

Donaldson, M. (1978b) Article in *Times Educational Supplement*, 28.4.78.

Doughty, P., Pearce, J., Thornton, G. (1971) *Language in Use*, Edward Arnold, London.

Du Boulay, B., O'Shea, T. (1976) 'How to Work the LOGO Machine', D.A.I. Occasional Paper No. 4, Department of Artificial Intelligence, University of Edinburgh.

Du Boulay, B., O'Shea, T., Monk, J. (1981). 'The Black Box Inside the Glass Box: Presenting Computing Concepts to Novices', *International Journal of Man-machine Studies*, **14**, 237—249.

Du Boulay, J. B. H. (1978) 'Learning Primary Mathematics Through Computer Programming', Ph.D. Dissertation, Department of Artificial Intelligence, University of Edinburgh.

Finlayson, H. (1985) 'Logo, Mathematics and Upper Primary School Children'. Unpublished Ph.D. thesis, University of Edinburgh.

Flavell, J. H. (1963) *The Developmental Psychology of Jean Piaget,* Van Nostrand Reinhold Company, New York.

Flower, L. S., Hayes, J. R. (1979) 'A Process Model of Composition', ERIC Report ED 218 661.

Flower, L., Hayes, J. R. (1981) 'PLans that Guide the Composing Process' in *Writing: the Nature, Development, and Teaching of Written Communication,* J. R. Donovan, B. W. McClelland (Editors), N.C.T.E., Urbana, Illinois.

Frase, L. T. (1980) 'Computer Aids for Text Editing and Design', Paper presented at the annual meeting of the American Educational Research Association, Boston, April 1980, Bell Laboratories, Piscataway, New Jersey.

Gaines, B., R., Facey, P. V. (1975) 'Some Experiences in Interactive System Development and Application', *Proceedings of the IEEE, 63,* No. 6.

Gleitman, L. R., Gleitman, H., Shipley, E. F. (1972) 'The Emergence of the Child as a Grammarian', *Cognition, 2,* 137—163.

Golub, L. S., Fredrick, W. C. (1971) 'Linguistic Structures in the Discourse of Fourth and Fifth Graders', Technical Report No. 166, Wisconsin Research and Development Center for Cognitive Learning, University of Wisconsin.

Halliday, M. A. K. (1967) 'Linguistics and the Teaching of English', in *Talking and Writing,* J. Britton (Editor), Methuen, London.

Halliday, M. A. K., Hasan, R. (1976) *Cohesion in English,* Longman, London.

Harpin, W. (1976) *The Second R,* George Allen and Unwin Ltd., London.

Harris, R. J. (1965) 'The Only Disturbing Feature'. *The Use of English, 16,* 3, 197—202.

Harrison, C. (1983) 'English Teaching and Computer-assisted Simulations', in *Exploring English with Microcomputers,* D. Chandler (Editor), Council for Educational Technology, London.

Humes, A. (1983) .The Composing Process: a summary of the research', ERIC Report ED 222 925.

Holbrook, D. (1961) *English for Maturity,* Cambridge University Press, Cambridge.

Howe, J. A. M. (1979) 'Learning Through Model Building', in *Expert Systems in Human and Artificial Intelligence,* F. Klix (Editor), Deutscher Verlag, Berlin.

Howe, J. A. M., O'Shea, T., Plane, F. (1979) 'Teaching Mathematics Through LOGO Programming: an Evaluation Study', Proceedings of I.F.I.P. Working Conference on C.A.L., London.

Hunt, K. W. (1965) 'Grammatical Structures Written at Three Grade Levels', N.C.T.E. Research Report No. 3, Champaign, Illinois.

Inhelder, B., Piaget, J. (1958) *The Growth of Logical Thinking from Childhood to Adolescence,* Basic Books, New York.

Johns, T. (1983) 'Generating Alternatives', in *Exploring English with Micro-computers,* D. Chandler (Editor), Council for Educational Technology, London.

Kahn. K. M. (1975) 'A LOGO Natural Language System', LOGO Working Paper No. 46, Massachusetts Institute of Technology, Cambridge, Mass.

Katz, J. J., Fodor, J. A. (1963) 'The Structure of a Semantic Theory', *Language, 39,* 170—210.

Kidder, C. L. (1974), 'Using the Computer to Measure Syntactic Density and Vocabulary Intensity in the Writing of Elementary School Children', Ph.D. Dissertation, Pennsylvania State University.

Kidder, C. L., Golub, L. S. (1976) 'Computer Application of a Syntactic Density Measure', *Computers and the Humanities, 10,* 325—331.

Kintsch, W., Kozminsky, E., Streby, W. H., McKoon, G., Keenan, J. K. (1975) 'Comprehension and Recall of Text as a Function of Content Variables', *Journal of Verbal Learning and Verbal Behaviour*, **14,** 196—214.

Leavis, F. R., Thompson, D. (1933) *Culture and Environment*, Chatto, London.

Levin, J. A., Boruta, M. J., Vasconcellos, M. T. (1982) 'Microcomputer-based Environments for Writing: a Writer's Assistant', in *Classroom Computers and Cognitive Science*, A. C. Wilkinson (Editor), Academic Press, New York.

Loban, M. D. (1963) 'The Language of Elementary School Children', Research Report No. 1, N.C.T.E., Champaign, Illinois.

Malgady, R. G., Barcher, P. R. (1979) 'Some Information-processing Models of Creative Writing', *Journal of Educational Psychology*, **71,** 5, 717—725.

Mandler, J. M., Johnson, N. S. (1977) 'Remembrance of Things Parsed: Story Structure and Recall', *Cognitive Psychology*, **9,** 111—151.

Marcus, S. (1982) 'Compupoem: A Computer-assisted Writing Activity' *The English Journal, February 1982*, pp. 96—99.

Martlew, M. (1983) 'Problems and Difficulties: Cognitive and Communicative Aspects of Writing Development', in *The Psychology of Written Language*, M. Martlew (Editor), John Wiley and Sons, Chichester.

Miller, L. A., Heidorn, G. E., Jensen, K. (1981) 'Text critiquing with the EPISTLE System: an Authors' Aid to Better Syntax', AFIPS Conference Proceedings, Volume 50, AFIPS Press, Arlington, Va.

Milner, S. (1973) 'The Effects of Computer Programming on Performance in Mathematics', Paper presented at the American Educational Research Association, ERIC Report ED 076 391.

Moffett, J. (1968) *Teaching the Universe of Discourse.* Houghton Mifflin, Boston.

Muir, J. (1975) ' "Language in Use" in Use'. *Teaching English*, **8,** 3, 14.

Murray, D. M. (1980) 'Writing as Process: How Writing Finds its own Meaning', in *Eight Approaches to Teaching Composition*, J. R. Donovan, B. W. McClelland (Editors), N.C.T.E., Urbana, Illinois.

Newell, A., Simon, H. A. (1972) *Human Problem Solving,* Prentice Hall, Englewood Cliffs, N.J.

Papert, S. (1980) *Mindstorms: Children, Computers, and Powerful Ideas*, Harvester Press, Brighton.

Protherough, R. (1983) *Encouraging Writing,* Methuen, London.

Quillian, M. R., (1966) 'Semantic Memory, Report AFCRL—66—189, Bolt, Beranek, and Newman Inc., Cambridge, Mass.

Rubin, A. (1980) 'Making Stories, Making Sense', *Language Arts*, 285—298.

Rumelhart, D. E., Lindsay, P. H., Norman, D. A. (1972) 'A Process Model for Long Term Memory' in *Organisation and Memory,* E. Tulving, W. Donaldson (Editors), Academic Press, New York.

Searles, J. R., Carlsen, G. R. (1960) 'English', in *Encyclopaedia of Educational Research*, Macmillan, New York.

Sharples, M. (1978) 'Poetry from LOGO', D.A.I. Working Paper No. 30, Department of Artificial Intelligence, University of Edinburgh.

Sharples, M. (1979) 'Using a Computer to Develop Written Style', D.A.I. Working Paper No. 54, Department of Artificial Intelligence, University of Edinburgh.

Sharples, M. (1983) 'The Design of a User-friendly System' in *The Computer Revolution in Education: New Technology for Distance Teaching*, A, Jones, E. Scanlon, T. O'Shea (Editors), Harvester Press, Brighton.

Slobin, D. I. (1971) *Psycholinguistics,* Scott, Foresman and Co., Glenview, Illinois.

Sloman, A. (1984) 'Beginners need Powerful Systems', in *New Horizons in Educational Computing,* Yazdani, M. (Editor), Ellis Horwood, Chichester.

Smith, E. B., Goodman, K. S., Meredith, R. (1970) *Language and Thinking in the Elementary School,* Holt, Rinehart and Winston Inc., New York.

Somers, N. (1980) 'Revision strategies of student writers and experienced adult writers', *College Composition and Communication,* **31,** 378—388.

Statz, J. (1973) 'Problem Solving and LOGO', in *Final Report of Syracuse University LOGO Project,* Syracuse University, New York.

Stewart, J. (1983) 'Does the Use of the Microcomputer Inhibit the Development of Language in Children?' in *Exploring English with Microcomputers,* D. Chandler (Editor), Council for Educational Technology, London.

Strunk, W., White, E. B. (1979) *The Elements of Style* (third edition). Macmillan, New York.

Thoulness, R. H. (1969) *Map of Educational Research,* National Foundation for Educational Research, London.

Wilkinson, A., Barnsley, G., Hana, P., Swan, M. (1980) *Assessing Language Development,* Oxford University Press, Oxford.

Winograd, T. (1972) *Understanding Natural Language,* Edinburgh University Press, Edinburgh.

Woodruff, E., Bereiter, C., Scardamalia, M. (1981) 'On the Road to Computer Assisted Composition', *Journal of Educational Technology Systems,* **10,** 2.

Zacchei (1982) 'The Adventures and Exploits of the Dynamic STORYMAKER and TEXTMAN, or How Johnny learns to understand what he reads', *Classroom Computer News,* **2,** 28—30.

Index